John Hartley

**Seets i' Yorkshire and Lancashire**

John Hartley

**Seets i' Yorkshire and Lancashire**

ISBN/EAN: 9783337148997

Printed in Europe, USA, Canada, Australia, Japan

Cover: Foto ©ninafisch / pixelio.de

More available books at **www.hansebooks.com**

# SEETS I' YORKSHIRE

## and LANCASHIRE.

---

By John Hartley.

---

# SEETS I' YORKSHIRE AND LANCASHIRE

GRIMES' COMICAL TRIP FROM LEEDS TO LIVERPOOL BY CANAL.

By JOHN HARTLEY,

AUTHOR OF "YORKSHIRE DITTIES," "YORKSHER PUDDIN," "GRIMES' VISIT TO TH' QUEEN," &c., &c.

"HUMOR, A KINDLY LITTLE BEE,
MAKES LAUGHTER SWEET AS HONEY;
WHILE WIT IS LIKE A WASP, FOR HE
STINGS WHEN HE'D FAIN BE FUNNY!"

W. NICHOLSON & SONS,
26, PATERNOSTER SQUARE, E.C.,
AND ALBION WORKS, WAKEFIELD.

# Dedication.

TO MY BROTHER WILLIAM.
(OF DURBAN, PORT NATAL, SOUTH AFRICA.)

AS A SMALL TOKEN OF MY LOVE AND ESTEEM THIS LITTLE BOOK I DEDICATE.

"NOR DISTANCE NOR TIME CAN SEVER THE TIE THAT BINDS."

JOHN HARTLEY

| CHAPTERS. | PAGE. |
|---|---|
| First—Feelin' his way | 7 |
| Second—Cut and Dried | 17 |
| Third—Peter's Letter—Setting off | 28 |
| Fourth—Peter's Welcome | 38 |
| Fifth—Voyage begun—What they saw an' what they didn't | 49 |
| Sixth—A Sunday Halt | 59 |
| Seventh—Bingley Beauties | 71 |
| Eighth—Fun on a Fly Booat | 82 |
| Ninth—Puttin' on Style | 93 |
| Tenth—Skipping off to Skipton | 104 |
| Eleventh—Nelson and Burnley | 116 |
| Twelfth—Wandering on to Wigan | 127 |
| Thirteenth—Nearing the End | 134 |
| Fourteenth—Conclusion | 145 |

# SEETS I' YORKSHIRE AND LANCASHIRE.

### CHAPTER FURST.

FEELIN' HIS WAY.

SAMMYWELL GRIMES an' his old wife MALLY wor sitting i' ther cooasy little cottage, quietly rockin' i' ther cheers, lissenin to th' shaats an' laffin' din at th' childer wor makkin i' th' Fowld, as they rompt an' tummeld abaat, rejoicin i'th sunshine at had come to mak May-day worthy ov its name an' th' traditions connected wi' it.

Sammywell had been readin th' paper, an' he let it slide off his knee onto th' floor, an' heaved sich a heavy sigh wol Molly stops her knittin to see what wor to do.

"Praythee, what's th' matter wi' thi? Tha

luks as yonderly as if tha'd nobbut just wakkened aght ov a dream an' didn't know whear tha wor."

"It's noa dream, Mally, lass; it's a hard matter o' fact. Aw wor just thinkin what pleasurs rich fowk enjoy at th' poor can nivver hooap to have."

"Happen net. An' if they have, they've moor cares an' anxiety. At onnyrate, aw connot see at tha's mich to grummel abaat. If tha artn't contented tha owt to be. If ther's owt at tha needs it's summat to do, for aw connot mak aht ha a chap can be satisfied to spend sich a life as tha does. Tha aits weel an' sleeps weel, an' tha drinks an' smooks moor nor does thi onny gooid, tha must admit that. Awm feeard sometimes when aw hear thi grummelin 'at summat may happen to thi for a punishment."

"Aw think aw've getten punishment enuff wi' havin thee, for tha nivver seems to sympathise wi' me. Aw think sometimes 'at aw made a sad mistak i' mi young days."

"Well, whether tha did or net, aw know one 'at did, for if awd nobbut had sense to wait asteead o' gettin wed when aw did aw should ha been ridin abaat i' mi own carriage, like a reel lady,—an' ther's nubdy knows it better nor thee. But what's upset thi nah? Tha's getten a skinful o' rooast beef an' yorksher puddin, an' tha's plenty o' bacca i' th' box, an' a pint pot at thi elbow at tha's nobbut just emptied."

"Awm nooan blamin thee, net aw marry! It isn't thy fault at tha cannot understand it. A chap wi' a mind like mine wants summat moor nor aitin an' drinkin an' sleepin. A pig wod be satisfied wi' that, but awm nooan a pig. Aw want summat moor elevatin;—summat to occupy mi brain."

"It willn't tak mich to do that, if that's all tha wants, but be careful tha doesn't find it too mich to do, for tha wor allus rayther waik i' th' top end; but if that's all, tha can sooin find summat, for ther isn't a bit o' kinlin wood for mornin, an' aw connot bide to chop it. It'll find thi summat to do for an haar or two for its as hard as nails. Awr Hepsabah sed when shoo saw it, 'at if ther wor nivver a foir kinneld i' their haase until shoo chopt it, they'd have to goa withaat for ivver an' a day longer."

"Tell awr Hepsabah to mind her own consarns an' shoo'll have plenty to do. But that's nawther here nor thear, but aw've just been readin abaat a lot o' theas rich fowk gooin yottin durin th' hot weather, an' here have aw to stick i' this smutherin hoil whear ther's hardly a breeath o' air stirrin! It isn't reight! Th' wealth isn't fairly divided or it wodn't be soa."

"Aw dunnot know what tha means bi 'yottin,'

but aw suppooas its some sooart ov a rant, an' aw think tha's been at that caper oft enuff. An' as for brass bein fairly devided, happen it isn't, for ther's monny a one livin abaat here 'at ud be thankful for a share o' what tha's getten. Awm sewer ther's awr Hepsabah's husband——"

"Shut up! Awr Hepsabah's husband's nowt to me! If he wants moor nor he's getten he mun haddle it th' same as aw've had to do."

"Thear tha gooas agean. If a body spaiks to thee its wrang. But if tha wants to goa 'yottin,' as tha calls it, put thi hat on an' yott; nobbut mind an' be back i' gooid time an' dooant keep thi drinkin waitin."

"Tha doesnt know what yottin is. A yott is a sooart ov a ship. It gooas sailin ovver th' salt seah; an' fowk goa sailin abaat throo' one place to another, seein all sooart o' fresh countries an' fresh faces."

"Oh! that's it is it! Well, aw think tha's seen as monny fresh faces as is likely to do thi onny gooid. Its abaat time tha sattled daan an tuk a bit moor nooatice o' some o' th' old faces. Aw see what tha'rt drivin at. Tha wants a excuse for another spree; that's what tha'rt after. Tha'd like to goa away for another month or two an' leeav all thi kith an' kin behund, an' then send to me for th' brass to fotch thi back! But tha's play'd that trick once too oft! An' as sewer as my name's Mally, if tha gooas agean tha may stop, for aw'll nivver send for thi back, an' tha'll find noa hooam here when tha comes, for aw'll sell up stick an stump an' goa live wi' awr Hepsabah! Awm nooan beholden to thi! Tha knows that! Ther's monny a one at'll be be rare an' glad to ha me if tha'rt stall'd on me."

"Hold thi whisht, do! Tha knows aw should nivver think o' sich a thing as gooin withaat thee. But its a thing 'at's unpossible. Theas yotts belang to rich fowk 'at nobbut goa an' tak a few o' ther own friends wi' 'em."

"Then its noa use thinkin onnymoor abaat it. But aw do agree wi' thee i' thinkin it's a shame 'at two daycent fowk like us, at's tewd as we have, an' dooant owe onnybody a penny, connot have as mich pleasur as other fowk. But tha'll happen be able to drop on a gooid second hand yott someday, an' then we can shew 'em. We're nooan short ov a paand or two, an' we'st ha th' divvy throo th' Co-op' in another wick or two."

"A'a, Mally lass! Some o' theas yotts cost hundreds o' thaasands o' paands: an' we couldn't spare enuff to buy a cockbooat. Th' fact is aw can hardly fashion to ax thi for th' price ov another pint, tho' this sudden spell o' warm weather maks me awfully dry."

"Nay, net it! Th' warm weather's nowt to do

wi' it. Tha wor born dry an' my belief is 'at tha'll be dry to th' end o'th' chapter. Ther's noa fear o' thee ivver deein wi' th' diabetus, tho' whear tha puts all tha swallers is beyond my calkilation. Awm just gooin to put th' kettle on to mak a sup o' teah, an' if tha connot wait wol its ready, tha knows whear th' sink is, an' tha mun let watter fit thi."

"Teah! It seems to me tha can live o' teah! It's suppin soa mich slop 'at's turnin thi skin as yoller as a guinea. Onnybody'd think to luk at thi 'at tha'd getten th' Jooanas."

"Wod they? But aw'll let thee know at ther isn't another woman tha can mention 'at's a skin like mine, at hawf my age! If awd sich an' old leather face as thee awd be shamed to put it aght o'th' door! It's a pity to waste sooap an' watter on it for it'll tak a scaarin stooan an' scrubbin brush to alter it! It's as awr Hepsabah says—"

"Havent aw tell'd thee, time an' time agean, 'at aw care nowt abaat what Hepsabah says? Tha needn't get narky abaat it. Thi face suits me weel enuff as it is, an' aw wor nobbut warnin thi net to do owt to spoil it. Aw know what it is tha needs. Tha caars i' th' haase too mich, an' tha works too hard. It's scandlus for a woman 'at's getten to thy time o' life to be bendin ther back ovver a peggy tub an' gooin daan o' ther knees to scaar th' flag stooans, to say nowt abaat ironin an' cookin an' bed makkin! Ther's noa reason in it! An' what's moor, ther's noa cashion for it. Aw dooant want to interfere wi' th' management o'th' haase, but aw see plain enuff aw'st be foorced, for tha willn't, an' as sooin as aw've getten mi drinkin aw'll set off an' see if aw connot find a strong likely lass to come an' live wi' us, an' do th' hardest pairt o'th' wark, an' then tha'll be able to get weshed an' donned like other wimmen, an' sit i' th' rockin cheer wi' thi hands befoor thi throo morn to neet. We can affoord it, an' we'll have it."

"Sammywell!"

"It's noa use sayin Sammywell! It's time for a alterashun an' ther's baan to be one. Bless mi life! awm war off nor a widdy."

"Sammywell, aw think——"

"It's all th' same to me what tha thinks, aw tell thi aw've been stall'd o' this way o' carryin on for a long time, an' if tha hasn't sense to know what's gooid for thisen its time aw shewd thi. Aw'll have a young woman i' th' haase afoor aw goa to bed to-neet!"

"Well, but, Sammywell,—just lissen to reason. Nah tha knows we've noa convenience i' this haase for onny young woman. Shoo couldn't caar up all th' neet, an' ther's nobbut one bed i' th' place, an' tha'd hardly expect us to give up awr bed for a stranger."

"Connot ta borro one o' Hepsabah's? Shoo'd think nowt abaat commin for awrs if shoo wanted it."

"Awr Hepsabah's nooan to lend. But that's nawther here nor thear. Shoo'd want some wage, an' summat to ait, an' awm sewer shoo'd mak moor wark nor shoo'd do. It's varry thowtful on thi to mention it, but its impossible. But here, sithee, goa an' fotch thisen a pint, for that kettle doesn't seem as if it wor likely to boil for a while, an' then when tha's getten it we'll tawk abaat this yottin. Its just struck me 'at it can happen be managed after all, for tha happen needs a bit ov a change, an' awd a deeal leever see thee sailin off nor awd have onny young woman coom sailin in here."

"Why, lass, ov coorse thart th' mistress i' thi own haase, an tha'll be like to suit thisen, but tha knows aw wor allus praad o' thi gooid luks, an aw dooant think tha's faded a bit. Aw nobbut want thi to be careful o' thisen, that's all."

---

"A'a, dear! aw think ther nivver wor a woman at had to deeal wi sich a chap as mine. Aw've to humour him war nor a child. But then aw shouldn't complain, for he's as gooid as gold, an aw dar say he does feel it to be tryin to caar here thro wick end to wick end an have nowt to do. That's whear th' bother is! If he'd nobbut start on an do a bit o' summat he'd be able to get on better; but its noa use thinkin abaat that, for he's th' lazyest drooan aw ivver met wi' i' mi life! Aw connot tell what's come ovver him, for he worked like a slave for aboon thirty year, an' nah 'at he can live baat it its ommost too mich trouble for him to draw his own breeath. Aw wish aw wor a bit moor like him, but awst have to tew on to th' end. If aw wor foorced to sit i'th rockin cheer wi' mi hands i'th front on me as he tawks on, awst be ready for th' sylum in a wick. But here he comes."

"A'a, lass! but it is wut. Aw think aw nivver knew a Mayday like this,—its fairly swelterin."

"It is a scorcher reight enuff. Wol tha sups that an has a bit o' bacca aw'll just slip aght an see ha awr Hepsabah's gettin on, for shoo's weshin to day, an if th' kettle boils just lift it onto th' hob."

---

"Th' old cratur's off agean. Its just like her. Shoo's nivver content unless shoo's medlin her heead wi' other fowk's consarns, as if shoo hadn't enuff ov her own. Aw dooant believe ther's sich another woman i' all Yewrup, to say nowt abaat Scotland an' Ireland! Aw wonder sometimes whativver wod become o' me if owt should happen to her. Pleeas God to let me goa furst. Aw wonder what nooation shoo's getten into her heead abaat yottin. Its varry little aw know abaat it an' shoo knows less. But it'll end in a bit ov a off o' some sooart aw'll be bun; for when shoo gets her studdyin cap on shoo generly manages to contrive summat. Aw believe shoo wor scared a bit when aw spake abaat bringin a young woman into th' haase. Aw didn't meean to vex th' old lass,—net aw marry!—but aw know what aw'll do!—Aw'll get th' drinkin ready wol shoo's aght, an' aw'll mak a bit o' tooast, an' aw'll put this bunch o' daffydaandillys on th' table, an' aw know shoo'll be suited. Shoo likes me to mak a bit o' fuss on her, an' why shouldn't aw?"

## CHAPTER SECOND.

#### CUT AND DRIED.

"A'A, SAMMYWELL, aw nivver thowt tha'd put thisen abaat to get th' drinkin' ready. Whativver made thi put that bunch o' daffies on th' table? Tha mun wait for me another minnet for aw couldn't think o' sittin daan to sich a spreead withaat puttin on mi new cap."

"Well, luk sharp befoor ivverything gets cold."

Mally went up stairs smilin all ovver her face, an' Sammy winked an' lukt booath suited an' sly. He tem'd aght th' teah an' put a extra lump o' sewgar into his wife's cup, an' shoo sooin joined him, lukkin as trim as blue ribbons an' white muslin could mak her.

"Sammywell," shoo sed, as shoo sipt her teah, "does ta remember th' time when tha furst put a bunch o' daffies on th' table?"

"Hi, lass, aw should think aw do. It's getten welny on for fifty year sin; an' aw remember

B

another thing, an' that is at th' daffies wor ommost all ther wor to put on th' table at that day."

"That's true enuff, lad, but aw dooant think ther's been monny young couples at started wedded life wi' leeter hearts. It nobbut luks like tother day, but ther's been a deeal o' changes sin then. Lads an lasses at wor bloomin then have withered away like th' daffydaandillys an' others are bloomin i' ther steead. Aw oft think abaat em when we sing,

> "The flowers of fifty summers gone,
>     The leaves that then wor green,
>   Have nothing left to look upon
>     To tell that they have been."

"True enuff lass,—true enuff; we've a deeal to be thankful for,—at leeast tha has whether aw have or net."

"An if tha hasn't aw should like to know why. But aw owt to have moor sense nor to harken to thi for tha hasn't a spark o' thankfulness i' thi whooal carkase."

"If tha wed me for a spark tha's fun aht thi mistak. Ther's noa spark abaat me."

"Except one, an' that's i' thi throit, an awm feeard tha'll nivver be able to sleck it."

"If tha tawks like that to me, Mally, awst nooan be soa ready at gettin thi drinkin ready another time."

"Tha can suit thisen. Nubdy axt thi to get it ready; an' if tha thinks awm gooin to caar here an' tak thy slurs withaat spaikin back, tha'rt mistaen."

"Well, let it drop, an' if tha's owt to say abaat yottin let's have it."

"Awm i' hawf a mind net to tell thi owt, an aw wodn't if aw didn't know at tha tawks just for tawkins sake. Its as awr Hepsabah says——"

"Aw willn't hear a word abaat what shoo says. If tha's owt to say, say it, an' dooant keep crammin awr Hepsabah daan mi throit, awm sick on it."

"Aw wor nobbut gooin to say at if tha wants to have a two-o-three day's yottin, as tha calls it, at aw can put thi into th' way at varry little expense. But tha clicks me up befoor aw've a chonce to spaik.

"Well, nah then, frame, an let's hear what it is."

"Ha monny year is it sin mi cussin Peter wor ovver to see us?"

"Why, let me see;—it'll be abaat five year sin aw reckon."

"Eeah,—If tha remembers he coom th' same day at awr Hepsabah's Jerrymiar started wi' th' mazzles. It'll be five year sin come Halifax thump Sundy, an' tha knows he's a captain is Peter, an' what's to prevent thee gooin a yottin wi' him? We've allus treated him weel when he's come here an' aw dooant think he'd deny a little thing like that. It's a easy matter to drop him a line. He allus puts up at th' 'Jolly Tar' when he's i' Leeds."

"By th' heart, lass! aw nivver thowt o' that. Peter 'll be just th' chap to give a body a tip. Aw'll write a letter to-neet an' ax him if he knows onnybody at's gooin; maybe, he can put me onto a gooid thing."

"Tha'd better ax him plain aght to tak thi wi' him on his next trip, an' then aw shouldn't feel soa uneasy wol tha wor away, for he'd luk after thi for my sake if he didn't for thi own."

"A'a, Mally,—tha tawks like a simpleton. Tha knows Peter isn't a reight captain, he nobbut sails throo Leeds to Liverpool on a canal booat. Aw want to sail on th' salt watter."

"It isn't a question ov what tha wants Sammywell, its what tha can get. Tha'll find ther's booath salt an' sewgar i' that canal, an' moor beside, an' whether or net, aw think its moor suitable for a chap o' thy years to be steady when thart away throo hooam, an' tha'll be a deeal steadier on th' canal nor tha will if tha gooas tossin abaat on th' seah, whear tha'll varry likely get shipwrecked an' cast on a desolate hyland where tha'll have nubdy to darn thi stockings an' set thi buttons on."

"But tha knows, lass, aw could walk to Liverpool i' less time nor it'll tak to goa in a canal booat. Its twice as far bi canal as it is bith railway."

"Soa mich the better! Tha's nowt else to do, an' tha mud as weel be ridin on th' canal as caarin whear tha art; an' awm sewer tha'll see moor between Leeds an' Liverpool nor tha'll see between Liverpool an' New York, an' if tha should fall ovverbooard an' get draand, we should be able to fotch thi hooam an' put thi away nice an' comfortable, an' that'll be better nor havin thi swallerd up wi' a whale an' nivver knowin what had come on thi; for if a whale once swallers thee it'll nooan do as it did wi' Jooanah an throw thi up agean, unless tha disagrees wi' it same as tha does wi' ivvery body else at's tryin to do thi a gooid turn."

"Aw dooant know ha it is, but if ivver aw tawk abaat settin off a bit tha allus begins to speculate on me commin back deead. One wod think at aw wor i'th habit o' dooin soa. But hasumivver, it seems at tha's made up thi mind at if aw goa at all aw mun goa wi' Peter, soa it shall be as tha says if we can shap it. Aw should think Peter harbors noa ill feelin towards me nah altho' aw did put his nooas aght when he coom smellin after thee. He seemed to tak it varry hard for a bit, but he little knows what he missed."

"Happen he doesn't, but he knows what aw've hit; for tha needn't think tha can goa on as tha does an' shut ivverybody's een up! He's a deeal better principled chap nor some at's had better luck, an' if he'd getten a wife sich as aw could mention he'd nooan be ridin on a canal booat to-day."

"Aw believe thi, lass,—he'd ha been ridin in a heearse long sin."

"It's noa use thee thinkin at tha can aggravate me for tha connot, an' if *tha* thinks sich remarks is seemly, *aw* dunnot. But aw've sed all awm baan to say an' wish awd nivver mentioned his name; an' aw nivver wod ha done if it hadn't been for awr Hepsabah sayin at if tha'd get aght o'th' gate for two-o'-three days shoo'd come an' help me to cleean daan, an' it should ha been done a month sin, but ther's noa dooin owt when tha'rt hallockin araand."

"Why, lass, aw think aw owt to be shamed o' misen, but tha mun tak noa nooatice. Tha knows it's nobbut a way aw have. Nah, if tha can manage to keep thi clapper still for abaat five minnits aw'll write to Peter an' tell him tha sends thi kind love, an' that'll suit him whether its true or net."

"Tha's noa need to mention my name for

aw've noa love to send, aw've little enuff for misen."

---

"Nah, lissen to this—

"'To Captain Peter Onion Esq.'"

"Well, if thar't gooin to insult him th' furst thing aw think tha'd better net write at all."

"Why, isn't that reight?"

"Noa, it isn't! An tha knows it isn't! His name's Garlick, an' his father's befoor him wor Garlick!"

"That's soa, aw mun alter that. Whenivver aw think abaat his name it allus fotches th' watter into mi een wol awm safe to mak a mistak. Nah, lissen—

"To Captain Garlick Esq.
        *Canal Booat Driver.*

"*Dear Cussin,*—*My wife wants me to write to yo to ax if yo could help her wi' her cleeanin daan, hooapin yo are well as this leaves us at present, which you cau do bi takkin me aght o'th' gate till shoo's getten done, an' lettin me sail wi' yo on yor next voyage to Liverpool. Shoo wod ha liked to come asteead o' me but shoo's a varry kittle stummack an' being trubbled wi' corns an' nangnails shoo's net fit for mich walkin' at present.*

"*Let me know when yo expect to start an' if aw shall have to bring mi own grub an' ha monny stoppin places ther'll be an' if they've old licensed for awm trubbled wi spazms which Mally says is a besettin sin an' aw think soa too but aw try to put up wi' it for the flesh is willin tho the sperits waik.*

*so no more at present from*
*Your cussin (by marriage to Mally)*
*Sammywell Grimes.*"

Ha will that do think's ta?"

"It isn't for me to tell thee ha to write a letter for awm noa skollar misen, but some pairts seems sensible enuff, especially that abaat mi corns, an' that abaat bein his cussin bi weddin me. Aw think it'll do, an' nah tak it to th' pooast office an' when tha's had a bit o' bacca we'll get some supper an' get off to bed i' daycent time, for we'st net get mich sleep unless th' wind changes or we've a shaar o' rain, for it's swelterin."

"Tha'rt reight, lass, it's varry sultry, an' ther's nowt plays up wi' thee like missin thi sleep. Doesn't ta think tha'd happen sleep a bit better if tha had a little drop o' summat befoor tha gooas to bed? Tha knows tha's getten to tak care o' thisen, for aw couldn't set off an' leeav thee if tha ailed owt."

"Aw dooant daat but what it wod help me to sleep, but aw dooant like to get into th' habit o' takkin sich stuff, but aw suppooas tha can do wi' a drop?"

"Why, tha knows aw nivver enjoy owt at sooart as weel as when tha'rt havin some. If tha likes to let me bring a sup aw'll join wi' thi."

'Here tha art sithee—be sewer an' bring th' reight change back an' dooant be long."

---

Sammywell worn't long, but when he put a pint bottle o' whisky on th' table, an' emptied an aance o' bacca into his box Mally sighed, shook her heead, held aght her hand for th' change, an' sed nowt.

"Nah this is summat like," sed Sammy, " aw dooant envy th' queen on her throoan when awm sittin anent thee an' ivverything at man can wish for within raik. Aw dooant care mich whether Peter answers mi letter or he doesn't. Awm nooan badly off wi' things as they are."

"Tha'll be content enuff until th' bottle's empty, but if tha thinks we can affoord to keep on at this racket tha'rt wrang, for spendin brass at this rate is th' way to th' poor haase i' quicksticks."

"Well, gie ovver grummelin, lass, an' lets mak th' best o' things as they are. What says ta if aw sing thi a song?"

"Suit thisen,—ther's nawther ale nor milk i'th' cellar, soa tha connot harm owt."

" Well, then here gooas,—

    Th' sun shone breet at early morn,
        Burds sang sweetly on the trees;
    Larks wor springin from the corn,
        Openin blossoms sowt the breeze;
    Jockey whistled as he went,
        O'er the meadows wet wi' dew;
    In his heart wor sweet content,
        For his wants an' cares wor few.
    Dolly passed him on his way,
        Fresh an' sweet an' fair wor she;
    Jockey lost his heart that day,
        To the maid ov Salterlee.
            Jockey an' Dolly
            Had allus been jolly,
Till Love shot his arrow an' wounded the twain;
            Their days then pass sadly,
            Yet man an' maid madly
In spite ov the torture they nursed the sweet pain.

    Sin' that day did Jockey pine;
        Dolly shyly kept apart,
    Still shoo milk'd her willin kine,
        Tho' shoo nursed a braikin heart.
    But one neet they met i' th' fold,
        When the mooin did breetly shine
    Jockey then his true love told,
        As he axt "will't thou be mine?"
    Tears ov joy filled Dolly's e'en,
        As shoo answered modestly;
    Dolly nah is Jockey's queen,—
        Th' bonniest wife i' Salterlee.

Jockey an' Dolly,
Are livin an' jolly;
May blessins for ivver attend i' ther train;
Their days they pass gladly,
Noa moor they feel sadly,
For ther hearts are for ivver bound fast i' Love's chain.

"Nah what's ta think abaat that?"

"Aw think it's abaat time to mak a sideashun an' get off to bed."

"All reight, lass;—just as tha's amind."

## CHAPTER THIRD.

#### PETER'S LETTER—SETTING OFF.

NEXT day Sammywell wandered abaat as if he wor lost. Mally sed he lukt war nor a old hen i'th meawt. He couldn't sattle to owt an' he didn't know whether to be pleased or grieved abaat writin to Peter. Time hung heavy on his hands an' he wor glad when th' day wor ovver an' he could goa to bed agean an' sleep an' forget all abaat it for a while. But he had some queer dreeams. Once or twice his wife had to wakken him. Once he wor dreamin he wor seah sick an' when he wakken'd he stuck to it until Mally gate up an' mixed him a dooas ov his favorite phisic. Then he fancied he wor shipwrecked an' cast ashore at Saltaire whear he couldn't get owt to sup except watter, an' i' tryin to hoist a signal ov distress he hoisted Mally aght o' bed an' raised a storm at tuk some time to sattle. Mornin seemed as if it wod nivver come but at last he fell into a dooaz an' didn't wakken agean until th' braikfast wor ready. Befoor they'd finished th' meal, th' pooastman coom an' sewer enuff ther wor a letter throo Leeds.

Sammywell oppened it an' Mally put on her spectacles soas shoo could hear better. This is what it sed.

"*Dear Cussin,*

*Come an' bring as mich grub as yo like. or if you cannot come send th' grub.—Meet me at th' 'Jolly Tar' next Setterdy mornin. It's agean arders to tak onny passengers, but tha can come as commodore. Bring a spyglass wi' thi an' some bacca an' a box o' matches.*

*Give my love to Mally an' tell her shoo's net to freeat abaat thi gettin draand becoss tha wor born to dee aboon heigh watter mark, but if owt should happen to thi shoo needn't be a widdy aboon a wick, an' a change mud happen cure her corns. Hopin tha'll behave thisen an' net disgrace thi cussin (which tha nivver wod ha been if Mally'd had onny gradely wit,) aw remain*

*Thy lovin relation*
*Captain Peter Garlick.*

*P.S. Tha'd better bring a tumbler glass as weel as a spyglass, an' if thart takkin this trip for th' sake ov a change be sewer an' bring some change i' thi pocket or tha may be disappointed. Better bring a bunch o' kays wi' thi to oppen th' locks wi. Tell Mally shood better have a poleeceman ready to tak thi i' charge at th' far end. Dooant bother abaat insurin thi life it isn't worth th' expence.*

*Good bye.*

"Well! That's the degger! What does ta think o' sich a letter as that? Aw'll see him far enuff befoor aw'll goa after gettin sich a letter as that! He can tak his old swilltub ov a booat an shove it i' pop for owt aw care! Its a reight daan insult—That's what aw call it!"

"Why, Sammywell, awm sewer it saands to me like a varry cussinish sooart ov a letter. Tha sees he doesn't disown thi tho' he knows thi soa weel, an' awm sewer he's gien thi some gooid advise. Aw can trust thee wi' Peter."

"That may be;—but whether its safe for me to trust misen wi' Peter is another matter."

"He says he'll mak thi into a commodoor, an' sewerly that's worth summat."

"He's moor likely to mak me into a battledoor to my way o' thinkin! But if he thinks he can laik at shuttlecock wi' me he's mistaen. Aw dooant believe he wants me to goa at all, but aw'll goa just to spite him! An if aw catch him playin onny hanky panky tricks wi' me aw'll repooart him to th' furst lord o'th admiralty aw meet. Get that seah chest o' mine looadened an' find me some clooas fit for a commodoor, an' gie me some brass to goa an' buy a spy glass, an' aw'll be off i'th mornin!"

"Aw think tha'd better goa an' see what one'll cost furst, but here's a shillin, an' see at tha doesn't spend it all."

"Ha does ta think awm gooin to get a spy glass for a shillin? Why it'll cost a paand at th' varry leeast."

"Then tha mun borrow one, or else do withaat spyin. Awr Hepsabah bowt a lukkin glass last setterdy neet for a shillin, it wor a crackt en, that shall be true,—but if its gooid enuff for her awst think a shillin spy glass should sarve thee weel enuff."

"But this cussin Peter says———"

"Aw tak noa nooatice o' what Peter says. He thinks we're made o' brass. He may be a navigator but he's noa calkilator. He's a reglar old salt."

"A sooart ov salt Peter aw reckon. Well, aw tell thi what we'll do. Tha shall get donned an' we'll goa together, an' then tha'll see for thisen."

"All reight, aw'll be ready in a minnet."

Together they set off an' Mally made straight for a popshop for shoo thowt shoo'd get one cheaper thear. Th' chap at kept it wor sometime befoor he could mak aght fairly what wor wanted but at last he tummeld to it.

"Oh!" he sed, "Its a talescope yo want! Aw've just the varry thing far yo. Aw've one here at Nelson used at th' battle o' Watterloo.

Its as gooid as new barrin it wants a glass in. Its rail mahogny an' brass, aw'll awarrant it to fell an ox withaat splittin. Yo can have it cheap. Its happen a bit old fashioned but its better for that. Its like th' mistress thear, its better ivveryday its kept. Just wait wol aw shak th' muck aght on it an' then yo can try it."

"Why, Sammywell," sed Mally, as shoo examined it, "awd noa nooation they wor as big as this. Tha'll want a little lad to hug it for thee. Its ommost as big as them secondhand legs ov awr Hepsabah's at her husband's made a mangle aght on. What's price on it, maister?"

"If yo tak it just as it is, it'll be five shillin, but if yo want a glass puttin in it'll be tuppince extra."

"Nah, Sammywell, what does ta say? pleeas thisen, tha knows its nooan for me."

"Well, aw think it'll do. Its ommost a yard long when its pooled aght to th' full, an' aw dooan't think at five shillin a yard is dear for a talescope. If this slidin piece wor made fast an' it wor turned thick end up it wodn't mak a bad peg-leg. Aw think it'll do furst rate."

"But willn't ta pay th' extra tuppince to have a little winder put in at that end?"

"Nay, aw dooan't think its worth while;—aw can see throo it as weel baght; an' beside tha can pack a gooid lot o' little things in it as it is, at'll come in handy on th' voyage."

"Well, then, we'll tak it."

Soa shoo paid for it an' Sammy tukt it under his arm an' they marched off. They'd nobbut gooan a few yards when Sammy stopt.

"Nay, lass," he sed, "awm nooan baan to walk throo th' street wi' thee i' that state. Why, tha artn't fit to be seen! Th' back o' thi shawl's covered wi' muck."

"Knock it off cannot ta?"

"It'll want a brush for that. It must be th' dust at's come aght o'th' spy glass. If onny o' awr chapel fowk should see thi nah, it ud fit 'em to tawk abaat for a month."

"Let's turn up this ginnel, then, an' tha can happen mak me luk seemly."

"Better goa into th' 'Duck an' Thunner' an' borrow a brush."

"Luk sharp then."

They wor sooin inside an' Sammy ordered two twopenoths an' a clooasbrush, "an' let 'em be hot?" he sed.

"Do yo want th' clooasbrush hot?" axt th' chap.

"Thee mind thi own business an' do as tha'rt tell'd," sed Mally.

They wor sooin sarved, an' Mally paid, but net withaat grummelin as it wor fourpince moor on

C

th' price o'th' spy glass. Sammy reckoned to mak a big fuss abaat brushin her daan, an' then sed shoo lukt a thaasand paand better for it, an' Mally wor soa suited to think at he'd soa mich pride abaat her 'at when he sed he thowt another twopenoth wod improve th' rooasies in her cheeks, shoo made noa objection, but put daan sixpence, an' let Sammy pocket th' change.

When they gat hooam shoo lost noa time i' gettin some Bristol brick an' some furnitur polish, an' in a varry short time th' old talescope lukt worth as mich agean.

Th' rest o' th' day wor occupied wi' alterin a suit o' clooas for Sammy so as to mak him luk moor fit for th' position ov a commodore. Shoo cut th' laps off his coit an' put a gusset into th' bottom ov each ov his britches slops, an' shoo put him a blue ribbon onto one o' Jerrymiah's strawbengies, an' bith time shoo'd done wi' him he felt sewer 'at nubdy could mistak him for a furst officer (o' th' sooart) whether he wor in a booat or a battle. What shoo put in his box he nivver bothered abaat after he'd seen a pund o' bacca an' a quart bottle full ov lotion for internal use only. Whether to feel shamed or praad Sammy didn't know, but as he lukt at hissen i'th' glass he felt sewer 'at he'd seen a pictur at lukt varry like him somewhear. Mally wor famously suited an' shoo declared he needed nowt but th' smell o' tar, an' a blue anchor marked o' one hand an' M. G. on tother to mak him luk as mich ov a sailor as Peter hissen. But when Hepsabah coom in an' saw him shoo rolled on th' floor as if shoo wor in a fit, an' shoo wor,— but it wor a laffin fit, an' if Mally hadn't taen her bi th' shoolders an' bundled her aght o'th' door ther'd ha been a smashed spy-glass an' th' probability ov a inquest.

Knowin at it wor th' last neet they'd spend together they tried to mak it as pleasant as possible, but they wor too anxious an' fidgetty to be comfortable. Sammy tried to sing "Rule Brittania" but he'd forgetten th' words an' when Mally struck up "The lass that loves a Sailor," her voice tremmeld soa wol shoo had to hold fast to th' wringin machine to steady it.

After a restless neet, when they'd booath done a deeal moor tossin abaat nor if they'd been abooard ship, they gate a gooid braikfast an' Sammy prepared for startin off, for he wor detarmined to be i' gooid time, an' he didn't care for Hepsabah seein him goa.

Mally lukt varry solemn but sed little; some-ha shoo felt moor anxious nor shoo had done formerly when he'd been gooin away.

"Well, lass, aw think all's ready nah. Tha

can send mi box to th' station. Old Billy sed last neet he'd come wi' his wheelbarro for it, soa aw think aw'll be gooin. Doesn't ta think awd better have a sup o' summat befoor aw start—summat just to keep mi sperrits up?"

"Tha can have nowt but a bottle o' pop, an aw think that'll be best for thi for tha'll want to have thi wits abaat thi when tha gets to Leeds."

"Tha knows pop nivver does for me. Th' last time aw tuk some it filled me wi' wind wol tha sed thisen 'at aw must ha been at a brass band contest. If that's all tha's getten aw'll goa dry-maath. Gooidby, lass!"

"Gooid bye, an' see 'at tha behaves thisen—tha knows what aw meean. An' if tha gets lost in a shipwreck come straight hooam, an' dooan't forget thi spy glass."

Bein sooin on i'th' mornin ther worn't monny fowk stirrin, but them 'at he did meet seemed varry pleased to see him, judgin bi th' way they smiled.

Billy wor sooin after him, an' he gate his ticket an' put his box into th' luggage van, an' wor gooin to get into a carriage when Billy says—

"How'd on, Sammy, this isn't th' reight train—this is for Leeds."

"Well, aw want to goa to Leeds."

"Ho! aw thowt tha wor gooin to Wakefield. Aw didn't know ther wor a sylum at Leeds. Does ta think tha'll ivver come back?"

"It'll be war for thee if aw do! Off tha gooas abaat thi business an' seek a sylum for thisen."

Th' whistle went — th' door slammed — an' Sammy wor off.

## CHAPTER FOURTH.

#### PETER'S WELCOME.

SAMMYWELL sooin saw at he wor creatin a bit ov a sensation, but then he argued 'What's th' use ov a chap dooin great things unless fowk know abaat it.' When he gat to Leeds he lukt for somdy 'at he could get to direct him to th' Jolly Tar, an' he saw a chap wi' a brass band on his cap neb an' he went to him.

"Why, maister," sed th' chap, "yo've comed to sooin. Th' horse show isn't wol Mondy."

"What's that getten to do wi' it? Tha doesn't tak me for a horse does ta?"

"Why, hardly;—but ther'll be donkeys thear as weel aw expect. But if yo want th' Jolly Tar, just goa aght o' that door an' follo thi nooas wol tha comes to a big gaslamp, then turn to thi reight an' then to thi left an' through a passage an' then ax. But be sewer tha doesn't run agean a poleeceman for they've getten strict orders to tak onnybody up 'at's seen huggin dangerous weapons."

"This is noa dangerous weapon,—its nobbut a spyglass."

"Oh! is that all? Aw thowt it wor a cannon. But tha'd better be careful, for if tha gets lost ther'll nubdy tak trubble to find thi unless ther's a reward offered, an' that's varry unlikely."

Sammy turned away i' disgust an' went to get his box, an' wol he wor wonderin ha' he'd have to hug it, a chap coom an' ax'd him "if he wanted his luggage takkin onnywhear?"

"Tha'rt th' chap aw want," he sed. "Aw want it takkin to th' Jolly Tar, whear aw've to meet mi cussin Peter. Ha mich will it cost?"

"Sixpence for th' box, an' sixpence extra if yo ride as weel, an' yo can suit yorsen whether yo treat me wi' owt or net."

"Call it ninepence an' it's a bargain."

"All reight. Come on." An' Sammy sooin saw his box put onto a handcart an' he climbed up an' sat on it. When they started off some o'th' shoeblacks an' match hawkers gave him a cheer, an' that raised his sperrits a bit, tho' he worn't quite sewer whether it wor becoss they wor glad to see him or thankful to be rid on him.

Ridin in a handcart worn't just as comfortable as he'd expected, an' he hadn't gooan far when he bawled aght "Howd on!" Th' chap ran th' wheel agean th' cawsey wi' sich a fullock wol Sammywell wor spared th' trouble o' gettin off, for he wor jolted into th' gutter, th' spyglass an' all, an' when he wor able to spaik he sed things 'at aw willn't repeat, an' puttin one hand under his coit tail, an' shakin th' spyglass wi' tother, he axt th' chap for his name. Th' chap didn't tremmel a bit but just lukt as sackless as if he'd upset a bundle o' shavins.

"My name's Ned Bringall, professional Baggage Banger at yor sarvice," he sed.

"Well, Mister Ned, does ta see owt like professional baggage abaat me 'at made thi chuck me into th' rooad i' that fashion? If it hadn't been for mi presence o' mind tha mud ha' been taen up for manslowter."

"They'd ha let me off at th' inquest. But what are yo baan to do? Aw can't stop here all th' day."

"Awm gooin to walk, an' tha can shak thi cart an' th' box into smithereens for owt aw care. They did reight to call thee Neddy, but they owt to ha' made thi ears a bit longer an' then we should ha' known."

They sooin coom to th' Jolly Tar, an' Sammy gave him a shillin, an' tuk his box inside.

"Is ther a chap called Captain Peter Garlick

here, 'coss he's my cussin if ther is?" he sed to a smart young woman 'at he met i'th' passage.

"Yes, there is," shoo sed, "but we want noa mewsic to-day."

"Aw've browt noa mewsic, mistress."

"Isn't that some sooart ov a trumpet?" shoo sed, pointin to his talescope.

"Noa, mun, aw believe it wor a spyglass when aw left hooam this mornin, but what it'll be befoor aw've had it mich longer aw cant tell. Yo see it pools aght i' this fashion."

"Dooant point it at me!" shoo skriked, "it mud happen goa off! Tak yorsen away!"

"Will yo be kind enuff to tell Captain Peter Garlick 'at ther's a gentleman wants to see him?"

"Whear is he?"

"He's here, mum,—it's me."

"Peter!" shoo bawl'd aght, "ther's some sooart ov a chap 'at says he's a gentleman an' wants to see thi."

"Its mi cussin Sammywell," Peter sed as he coom aght. "A'a, Sammywell! tha'rt just i' time. Come in an' sit thi daan, an' bring thi furnitur wi' thi. Let's have another hawf gallon mistress. This is him at wed mi cussin Mally 'at yo've heeard me tawk abaat. A grand lass shoo wor at that day, an' sensible too i' mooast things."

"An' is shoo livin yet?" sed th' mistress.

"Hi! shoo's weel an' hearty aw believe."

"It isn't to tell what some wimmen can put up wi'."

"Is yore husband livin yet, mistress?" axt Sammy.

"Nay, he's been deead a duzzen year or moor."

"He wor a varry sensible chap aw should fancy."

"He wor. An' as gooid as gold. If awd mi time to do ovver awd wed him agean."

"Happen net. He might have altered his mind."

Peter dragged him into th' tapraam an' pushed him into a seat. "This is old Grimes," he sed to his two mates 'at wor with him, "an' theas, Sammy," pointin to his chums, "are two friends o' mine. This is Throstle, an' this baat chin is Crammer. We're all gooin together an' aw think we'st be a nice quartett. Here's th' ale, soa seize howd o'th' pint an' sup."

Sammywell wor seldom backard at commin forrad when ther wor onny gooid ale stirrin, an' he drank all ther gooid health's an' then sattled daan to wait for th' next move.

Ther wor a gooid deeal o' laffin an' winkin bi Peter an' his mates, but Sammy reckoned to tak noa nooatice. Then Peter sed, "Aw see tha's getten dressed up for th' voyage, an' tha couldn't have come at a better time, for it'll be just like a picnic. We shall start this afternooin on a Fly booat 'at runs to Skipton, but we can get off just when we feel inclined, an' goa on bi onny other booat we can catch, for aw've getten orders throo th' main office at Liverpool. Tha mun understand 'at some woman wanted to send a birthday present to her dowter at Bootle, an' as shoo'd once lost a bundle 'at shoo'd sent bi train, shoo determined to send this carpet-bag full o' stuff bi booat, an' ha its happened nubdy can tell, but that's getten lost. Aw dooant know what wor in it, but it must ha been worth a gooid bit for shoo's played the hangment abaat it, soa aw've to goa an' see if aw can trace it. Soa tha sees we can awther ride or walk or tak th' train a bit, just as we fancy. We'st be sewer to own it if we see it, becoss its made o' red carpet an's been mended wi' black worset, an' one o'th' hannels is off, an' its directed to Abagail Cornstock to wait till called for, an' its waitin yet."

"That'll be varry nice,—but what mun aw do wi' mi box?"

"Oh, that 'll be reight enuff. We can carry that bit ov a consarn bi turns. Let's feel th' weight on it."

"This isn't it. This is nobbut a spy-glass. Mi box is i' th' passage. Tha sed awd to bring some grub an' bacca an' stuff."

"Eeah aw did, but aw didn't expect tha'd bring a kist full. Here, Throstle,—thee an' Crammer fotch it in here. We can happen leeten it a bit."

They sooin had it in an' on th' table, an' Sammy oppened it.

"Nah then," sed Peter, "th' captain furst allus. Let's see what ther is," an' he began to empty it. "Ham shank,—that's gooid! Tell th' mistress to bring some plates an' knives an' forks an' a oonion or two. Four teah cakes;—just one apiece. What's this? oh, aw see;—Two curran looaves an' a lump o' cheese—that'll do to finish off wi'. Bacca! as sewer as awm here! Aw'll tak care o' that misen.—Two boxes o' matches—tha can tak them, Throstle. Bottle o' pickles;— tell th' mistress we dooant want her oonions,— Eggs—a duzzen on 'em—boiled hard—shoo's a thowtful woman is Mally, an' aw allus sed soa. We can put them in us pockets. Butter,—enuff to start a shop,—an' what's this?—gently does it, —summat extra,—its lapt up i' a pair o' Sammy's stockins.—It is! aw thowt it wor! A bottle o' whisky as sewer as awm livin! Hands off! Captain furst yo know."

"It seems to me 'at th' captain *is* th' furst," sed Sammy, makkin a grab for th' bottle, "but whear does th' commodoor come in? Tha knows awm th' commodoor on this voyage."

"That's true. Well, mates, aw think th' commodoor should hug th' whisky, seein 'at we shalln't want it befoor neet, an' he can put it in th' talescope, it'll just abaat hold it. Ther's nowt else but clooas, an' they willn't be wanted wol we come back; soa shut it up an' tell th' mistress to put it i'th' cellar wol we call for it. An' tell her to bring in another hawf gallon an luk sharp wi' th' knives an' stuff for we're all clammin. Aw nivver knew sich a thowtful woman as mi cussin Mally. Aw wish shoo wor here just nah."

"If shoo wor tha'd wish tha wor somwhear else."

Ther wor noa time for moor tawk for th' mistress browt in th' ale an' th' plates, an' th' captain tell'd 'em all to draw up which they did, an' for th' next fifteen minnits ther wor nowt to be heeard but th' rattle o' knives an' forks. Onnybody to watch 'em wod ha thowt they'd been waitin for a wick, for when they'd done ther wor varry little left. But they booath felt an' lukt better for it, an' as sooin as ther pipes wor leeted Throstle struck up a song—

"What's the use ov worryin?
What's the use ov keer?
What's the use ov buryin,
Folks 'at's livin here?

> What's the use ov ketchin
>   Sorrers on the wing?
> Let um goa a-flyin—
>   Stretch yor necks an' sing."

An' he did stretch his neck an' his jaws too, but he wor nowt to compare wi' Crammer, for he didn't need to stretch his neck, for he seemed to be little else but neck throo his belly-belt up to his lips; an' when he tuk hold o' th' pint he nivver offered to drink but just oppened his face an' tem'd it daan, an' if yo wor cloise to him yo could hear it splash as it fell daan into th' cistern 'at he carried below. But they wor all feelin varry jolly, an' even th' mistress had a pleasant word for 'em ivvery time shoo filled th' jug.

But time wor creepin on an' Peter sed, "Nah, lads,—square up,—it's abaat time aw went to th' office for we've to start bi five o'clock an' we munnat be lat," soa he gate up an' gave hissen a shake (an' he wor summat to shake for he weighed abaat fourteen stooan,) he axt Sammy to let him luk at th' spy glass.

"Why," he sed, "its little moor nor th' case! Ther's noa lens in at one end."

"Noa, aw gate it cheaper on that accaant. Aw thowt as we worn't gooin on th' ooacean it 'ud happen do."

"It'll do furst rate, it couldn't ha been better. Tha'll be able to see thi way hooam throo it aw dar say. It'll just hold that bottle o' whisky." Soa they put it in.

"Nah, Crammer,—stir thisen an' try to luk like dooin summat even if tha doesn't feel like it. An' thee, Throstle! what's th' matter wi' thi? Tha luks hawf asleep!"

"Aw feel as if aw'd summat i' mi heead."

"Well, tha'd better ax th' mistress for a small tooith comb."

"It isn't aghtside. Its a cold or summat at aw've getten in it."

"Then its cold tha may be sewer, for tha'd nivver owt else in it. But wakken up an' let's be off."

They wor sooin ready an' started for th' office throo a paarin rain. Sammy wished he'd had his umberel, but he bethowt him 'at sailors didn't carry umberels on shipbooard an' he'd noa desire to set a bad example.

Peter wor a long time i'th' office, for ther wor a little stove in it, an' when he coom aght his clooas wor nice an' dry, but Sammy wor weet throo an' his straw-bengy hung raand his heead like a soft havvercake. Peter gave th' order "All abooard," an' led th' way, an' they wor sooin off.

"Sammywell," he sed, "tha'd better goa daan below aght o'th' weet."

"Is this th' cabin?" ax'd Sammy.

"That's th' state room," sed Peter. Sammy went daan but wor up agean in a few minnits.

"They do reight to call that a state raam," he sed, "aw've seen moor room but nivver as mich state. Awst be smoored."

## CHAPTER FIFTH.

VOYAGE BEGUN—WHAT THEY SAW AN' WHAT THEY DIDN'T.

SAMMYWELL wor booath surprised an' pleeased to find 'at th' Flybooat went bi steam, an' he wor surprised to see what a number ov booats ther wor,—some like his own an' some a vast deeal bigger, an' ther wor plenty gooin on all sides to interest him, an' he wor capt to see what big buildins they passed an' bridges they went under. "Aw've heeard fowk sing at "Leeds wor a seaport Taan, O," but awd noa idea 'at it wor as mich like one as it is. If th' watter wor nobbut a bit clearer an' th' smell net quite as strong, it wod be pleasanter." But a bit o' bacca improved matters, an' as th' rain nah wor nobbut a drizzle he lukt raand for a place whear he could sit comfortably, an' if it hadn't been for Peter commin nah an' then to tell him whear they wor an' what they wor passin, he'd ha' fallen asleep.

Hunslet an' Armley didn't interest him mich, but it didn't seem varry long befoor they coom i'th' seet o' grass an' green trees. It wor a varry dull sky an' darkness wor on 'em a deeal sooiner nor it should ha' been an' bi th' time Peter tell'd him 'at they wor near Kirkstall it wor too dark to see varry mich; yet he'd a fancy to see as mich as he could, an' th' quietness seemed grateful to him, soa he emptied his spyglass,—takkin care to put th' whisky bottle in his side pocket,—an' prepared to have a gooid squint at th' old abbey.

> "Like the lone wanderer who takes his stand
> On some tall cliff, with heavy, anxious breast,
> And looks far onward, o'er a weary land,
> For some green oasis of tranquil rest;
> So even I, in long expectant gaze,
> Hail with delight and unaffected glee,"
> Old Kirkstall, frowning through a muggy haze.

That's what Sammywell sed to hissen, an' he humbly begs Clarence Foster's pardon for dooin it. Clarence hasn't written mich, (moor shame on him!) but he's written that at'll live long after him an' all his patients are deead. Aw allus think abaat him when aw think abaat Leeds. An' ther wor another, a humbler worshipper of the muse;—Charley Kirby,—he's gooan to join that great majority whear his sweet singin is for other ears. He wor Nature's own lad! Monny a sweet song have aw heeard him sing, but at present aw can nobbut call one to mi mind, an for old memories sake aw'll try to give it,—tho' it isn't one ov his best.

> "Heather bells, sweet heather bells,
> Dancing in the woodland dells,
> O'er the moorlands and the fells,
> Heather bells, fair heather bells.
>
>> Oh! what joy to see you smile,
>> With such blithesome, winsome wile,
>> Ye a poet's heart beguile,
>> Heather bells, sweet heather bells.
>
> I will sit me down to rest,—
> Watch the pearls gleam on each crest,
> Till bright fancies fill my breast,—
> Heather bells,—sweet heather bells.
>
> "Heather bells,—fresh heather bells,—
> Much I love your soft toned knells;
> Whispering o'er the moss-grown wells,—
> Heather bells,—dear heather bells.
>
>> Most divine your faces are,
>> Shining like the evening star,
>> In the cloudless heaven afar,—
>> Heather bells—prized heather bells.
>
> From each eye such sweetness beams,
> Like pale moonlight on the streams,
> Where the water lily dreams
> Heather bells,—bright heather bells."

An' moor o'th' same sooart. Aw allus feel sad when aw think ov poor Charley,—he wor like a lot moor,—born to struggle an' deed at it.—Them at could appreciate him, couldn't help him, an' them 'at could ha' helpt him didn't know his worth.

"Well, this is the degger!" sed Sammy, as he tried his spy glass. "Aw believe this is a swindle! aw can see better withaat it nor wi' it."

"Ha con ta expect to see owt i'th' dark?" sed Crammer, "just wait wol aw strike a match." But when th' match flared up, all Sammy could see wor his talescope, soa he shut it up i' disgust, an' felt thankful to know th' old ruin wor thear,—whether it wor to be seen or net,—an' if it had nivver been o' mich use i' former days, he knew it had been th' meeans o' linin th' pockets o' some o' them 'at's allus smellin after plunderin th' public. All aw hooap is 'at they willn't carry on ther soa called "restoration" wol ther's nowt left to venerate. Col. North bowt it an' presented it to Leeds. All honour to him for his generosity!—but its a pity he didn't keep it. Th' next time aw pass it aw shall expect to see it whiteweshed, an' all th' winders glazed, an a sign on "To Let."

Peter coom to have a bit ov a tawk, an' Throstle an' Crammer sooin joined 'em. Throstle wor singin,

"Who'll have a ride on the silvery ocean?
Who'll have a ride on the silvery sea?" &c.

An' Crammer tried to put him aght wi' warblin,

"Her brow is like the snowdrift,
Her neck is like the swan."

"That's enuff," sed Peter. "Thy neck's like a horstritch, an' its as dry aw'll be bun. Aw must say 'at aw feel rayther pairched misen. Did ta throw that bottle ovverbooard, Sammywell?"

"Nay, aw didn't. If tha wants a drop tha can ax for it. Here it is sithee. Aw've just been tryin to get a luk at th' old abbey, but aw couldn't mak owt aght. Mun aw hand thi th' glass?"

"Noa, nivver heed. Aw seldom use a glass, aw mooastly sup aght o'th' bottle neck. Here, Throstle,—weet thi whistle an' pass it on to Crammer. Its a drop o' gooid stuff. Mally knows what's what."

"Aw dar say shoo does, but awst know what's watter, awm thinkin if aw dooant luk aght. Raik that bottle ovver here, Crammer," sed Sammy.

"Nah, mates;—" sed Peter, "dooant goa an' mak beeasts o' yorsen, an remember its Sammy's bottle, an' he wed a cussin o' mine."

When Sammy gate th' bottle back he smell'd at it to mak sewer 'at it had held whisky an' then he pitched it agean a sign pooast on th' bank side.

"What says ta, Sammy, as th' neets likely to be uncomfortable, if we stop at Shipley, an' then goa to Bradford an' have a gooid time?"

"Tha must be wrang i' thi heead aw think. Aw nobbut left Bradford this mornin, does ta think awm baan back to-neet? If awr Mally'd to find it aght shoo'd be malancholy! We'll stop at Shipley if tha's a mind. Awm gettin stall'd o' this consarn already. Ha far is it to th' far end?"

"Why its calkilated to be a hundred an' fotty four mile throo Leeds to Liverpool bi canal. It tuk a long time to mak it. It wor begun i' 1770, an' finished i' 1816."

"Does ta think at we'st ivver get to th' far end at th' rate we're gooin, becoss awm thinkin aw'st get aght an' walk."

"We shall be at Shipley directly an' then we'll get off an' call in at th' 'Sun' for a leck on, an' we can tak another booat when we feel like it."

"Aw begin to feel like it already. If this is *yottin* awd rayther have *trottin* even if it has to be shanks galloway."

> "Then a yottin we will go, brave boys,
> And a yottin we will go;
> We'll try all means and work all schemes
> To keep the poor man low."

Ov coorse it wor Throstle at wor makkin that

din. Sammy pooled his hat brim daan ovver his heead an' turned his coit collar up to keep it i' place, an' prepared to wait as patiently as he could for th' time when he could stretch his legs, an' his thowts wandered back to times long past, an' fowk who seemed to have dropt aght ov one's remembrance. What happy times ther used to be i' Bradford when kindred souls used to meet an' swap thowts, an' dream dreams, an' build hooaps at wor nivver roofed in,—but still left faandations on which others may raise a lastin temple to be admired when their names are forgotten. Whear is Annie Clough? Who doesnt remember her sweet, heart-touchin poems 'at used to soa oft grace th' columns ov th' "Observer" ov twenty-five years ago? Gifted as few are;—blessed bi nature wi' ivvery charm 'at mak's a perfect woman, an' to-day aw connot even find a copy ov her works. Aw may'nt know mich abaat poetry,—aw dooant suppooas aw do,—but aw know when another heart whispers i' tones 'at strike a chord i' mi own. Listen to this—

> "Please follow me,—just for a moment,
>     I'll show you a picture of Love;
> And of Faith so implicity Holy,
>     To be worth registration above.
> Step softly,—the hour is past midnight,—
>     The storm rages fearful and long;

Lightnings flash,—thunders roll,—winds whistle
  With a weird, relentless song.

Now come on your tiptoe,—gently,—
  Peep into that dainty room,—
There's a sweet, little white-robed figure,
  Standing out in relief to the gloom.
She pauses a moment, then swiftly
  Glides out through the open door,
Seeking a place of security,
  Fearing the thunder's roar.

Now, here is a spacious apartment,
  The fire is still burning, but low,
The door opens,—the little one enters,
  And steals into the bed so slow.
The sleeper starts up in amazement,—
  For the light is uncertain and dim,
And a head on the vacant pillow
  Is a sight long since strange to him.

"Who is this?" he cries out in wonder,—
  "It is only me,—papa,—
I was so afraid of the thunder,—
  But I'm safe where I know you are."
He folded the trembling cherub,
  With tears to his lonely heart;
And a prayer floated softly to Heaven,
  "Shield her, Father, when we must part."

Now this is my glorious picture,—
  A lesson to take let us try;
For we know we are safe from life's thunders,
  When our Heavenly Father is nigh."

If that isn't poetry aw dooant know what is. But its time to think abaat summat else, for

"We may live without poetry, music and art;
We may live without conscience, and live without heart;
We may live without friends, we may live without books,
But civilized man cannot live without cooks."

Sammywell wor quite ready to step ashore when Peter tell'd him they wor at Shipley. He wor stiff an' soor, an' he began to specilate abaat th' state he'd be in bith time he gate back hooam.

"Peter," he sed, "Are ta owt ov a hand at spetchin a chap's britches seeat?"

"Nay, Sammy, aw nivver heeard o' sich a thing. What's to do? Do they let th' watter in?"

"It seems to me as if they've let booath watter an' blisters in."

"O, tak noa nooatice o' that,—ther'll nubdy see it."

"But somdy can feel it if tha cannot."

"Dooant let Throstle here thi mention it, for if he does he'll mak up a song abaat it. What does ta think we'd better have to ait? Aw think some beefsteaks an' pickle an' breead an' a soop o' ale, (net mich—a gallon 'll do), owt to fit us but if tha'd rayther have owt else, spaik; tha knows th' commodoor pays—isn't that soa, Throstle?"

"It strikes me 'at yor havin me for th' mug. But tha knows, Peter, if aw wed thi cussin aw didn't wed thee an' all th' ragamuffins tha has trailin after thi. Aw'll pay mi share an' that's all aw shall do!"

"That's all aw want thi to do. Its a reglar thing on excursions o' this sooart;—Tha pays all when we're on shore an' aw find all when tha'rt abooard. Isn't that reight?"

"Oh, e'eah, that's all reight. Aw nobbut wanted to understand it."

"Come on in then an order what tha wants."

## CHAPTER SIXTH.

**A SUNDAY HALT.**

SAMMYWELL an' his party wor a sackless lukkin lot as they entered th' "Sun."

"Net another drop for onnybody to-neet!" sed th' maister.

"We didn't know it wor shuttin up time," sed Peter, "but yo see we're travellers."

"Awm glad on it. Th' sooiner yo travel an' th' better," an' withaat moor to do they wor hustled into th' street.

This wor a awkard predicament to be in, an' one aght o'th' lot wished he wor at hooam.

"Has nooan on yo onny friends i' theas parts?" sed Sammywell, "or are we to caar aght i' th' street all neet?"

"Blest if aw know what to do!" sed Peter, "let's leet a bit o' bacca an' sit on theas doorsteps wol we think matters ovver. Ther'll be noa moor booats up to-neet, that's a moral sartenty."

They'd hardly set daan when th' door oppened an' a chap in his shirt sleeves wanted to know "what they wor dooin thear?"

"That's what we want to know," sed Sammywell. "We're four poor sailor chaps 'at's getten wrecked on this desolate shore an' if awr Mally knew shoo'd rooar her e'en up."

"Aw dooant know what yo're Mally wor thinkin on to let thee aght. Isn't thy name Grimes?"

"It is, maister! Aw'll tak mi affydavey on it! Could yo tell us whear we can get a neet's lodgins? We're all daycent chaps, tha can see that."

"Come inside an' aw'll see what aw can do. It isn't mich aw can offer but it'll be better nor caarin aght i'th' weet."

When they'd all getten inside, th' chap lukt at 'em an' sed, "Sit yo daan. It's a gooid job th' wife an' childer's all i' bed. They'd ha been tarrified aght o' ther wits. But yor welcome to spend th' neet here, an' aw'll fotch up a drop o' hooam brew'd an' when yo've had yor bacca aw'll leeav yo."

Th' bacca an' th' beer didn't last long, an' after mendin up th' foir, th' chap left 'em to thersen to mak th' best on it.

Sammy tuk th' langsettle an' th' captain had th' rockin cheer, wol tother two ligged on th' hearthrug, an' varry sooin Sammy wor th' only one 'at wor wakken. He couldn't sleep, for his clooas wor damp an' his mind unsettled, an' he'd ha gien all th' brass he had in his pocket to ha been at hooam. He did think once or twice abaat gettin up an' startin off for Bradford, but he didn't want Hepsabah to laff at him. At last he sank into a dooaz an' when he wakkened he wor pleased to see th' sun shinin throo th' edge o'th' blind. He sooin raaised his mates an' they wor just gooin aghtside when th' maister o' th' haase coom daan.

"Nah then," he sed, "yor nooan gooin baght braikfast, yo can get nowt aghtside at this time i'th' mornin, but yor welcome to a bit o' cheese an' breead an' some moor hooambrew'd," an' wol he wor tawkin he wor puttin th' stuff on th' table, an' they didn't need invitin twice.

"Aw dooant know what they call thi," sed Sammy, "but tha'rt a Samaritan,— aw know that."

"Tha'rt mistakken, Sammy, for awm one o'th' Winterbothams."

"Well, tha may be a Winterbottom but tha's a warm heart, an' nah if tha'll tell us ha mich we owe thi for what we've had we'll pay thi, an' still feel i' thi debt; an' when aw tell awr Mally ha tha's takken us in shoo'll thank thi too."

"Yo've nooan been takken in as badly as

Mally wor when shoo tuk thee. Aw knew Mally long afoor tha did—we used to laik at makkin pob hoils together. Shoo wor a nice lass, an' fowk used to fancy shoo'd mak a gooid match, but ther's nivver noa accaantin for taste."

"Let's be off," sed Peter, "ther'll be a booat happen bi nah."

"Aw think yo'd better sattle daan for th' day if yo've nowt particlar to do. We can have a bit ov a walk nah, an' latter on we can goa to Shipley Glen an' have a nice quiet day."

An' soa it wor agreed. They went for a stroll an' famously they enjoyed it for th' air wor as sweet as new milk. Throstle started to sing "Hail smilin morn," but Sammy axt him if he knew what day it wor an' that stopt him.

Winterbottom showed 'em raand, takkin 'em up one street an' daan another an' they wor capt to see what a nice little taan Shipley wor growin into. Then they went daan to th' river Aire, an' th' tawk turned on to John Nicholson an' his sad end, (April 13th 1843.) Winterbottom pointed aght whear he'd crossed th' river, an' whear he wor faand deead, an' then they called to mind his "Genius and Intemperance," "The Drunkards' Retribution," "The Drunkard's portion," an' his seldom equalled, tho' little known "Poacher," an' spekilated on th' strange inconsistancy ov his life an' his labors, but as Bobby Burns says—

> "Then gently scan thy brother man,
>   Still gentler, sister woman,
>   For tho they gang a kenning wrang
>   To step aside is human.
>
> \* \* \* \* \*
>
>   Then at the balance let's be mute,
>     We never can adjust it;
>   What's done we partly may compute,
>     But we know not what's resisted."

We gat back to Winterbottom's befoor nine o'clock, an' after a rare tuck aght o' ham an' eggs we started for th' Glen. We'd a long walk but a pleasant en, an' aw must say 'at altho awd seen Shipley Glen monny a time befoor, awd nivver seen it when it lukt owt like as weel. May is th' month when its at its best. We wor all pratty weel tired an' a loll under th' trees wor a treeat.

Peter an' his chums wandered abaat leavin Winterbottom an' me to have a chat abaat old times.

"An' ha does Mally seem to be gettin on?"

"Well," aw says, "when aw left hooam to start o' this voyage——"

"Tramp, tha meeans."

"Well, call it what tha likes. Shoo wor just abaat as usual, an' aw darsay shoo'd ha come wi me, but tha sees shoo's getten soa fat wol shoo isn't able to get abaat as shoo used to. Mun, shoo's twice as big as shoo wor when aw gat her, an' sometimes awm feeard they'll be havin me up for bigamy or trigamy or summat. When shoo gets cross shoo's a varry heavy cross aw can assure thi; but considerin all things shoo mud be war."

"Well, we've all summat to sorrow abaat, but tha mun remember, if ther wor noa sorrow i' th' world ther'd be noa sympathy."

Takkin it all together we had a varry quiet, pleasant day. Booath Peter an' me felt fresher for it an' Crammer an' Throstle soberer. When we landed back at Winterbottom's, ther wor a gooid drinkin ready, an' after that we all joined i' singin some old psalm tunes, one o'th' lads playin a concertina 'at wor ommost as big as a drum, an' Mistress Winterbottom kept time wi' her rockin cheer. Throstle bell'd aght wol th' sweeat rolled off th' end ov his nooas, an' Crammer oppened his maath an' seemed to swallo it all wi' a relish.

Th' time coom when we mud mak a move, an' soa thankin 'em all for ther kindness we left 'em an' went daan to th' canal to see if ther wor onny signs ov a booat, an' as luck wod have it, ther wor one, but as it had some cargo to unship it wor net gooin on befoor mornin. Ther wor nobbut one man left i' charge an' as Peter knew him we all went abooard an' made ussen as comfortable as we could. Aw wor pratty weel tired an' sooin fell asleep, an' when aw wakkened we wor on us way to Saltaire. It wor a grand mornin an' as we wor sailin bi one horse paar, it seemed to me as if it worn't impossible to get to Saltaire befoor winter set in. Peter proved to be a gooid provider, an' altho' it wor rough an' ready it wor varry acceptable. When awd getten mi pipe aw wor varry mich tempted to get off an' walk, but aw thowt it ud luk shabby to leeav 'em, an' they all seemed contented enuff. It felt a bit like "The days we went a gipsyin a long time ago," an' as aw remembered it wor sed at "Time wor made for slaves," aw determined to be free for a time. In spite ov th' snail gallop we seemed to be gooin at, we gate to Saltaire abaat ten o'clock i'th' fornooin, an' as ther had to be another stop, we decided to get off an' stretch us legs a bit an' have a luk raand. Ivverybody knows what a nice cleean, dry place Saltaire is. Sir Titus Salt left a grander monument behund him i' that model taan nor onny at futur generations can raise to him. We had a walk throo th' park an' then admired th' buildins ah' th' factories whear thaasands find th' means ov makkin a livin. Aw missed a few old faces, for tho' th' taan lukt mich as it did when aw last visited it, th' fowk keep changin.

Old Abraham Oldroyd wor noa longer thear wi'

E

his quiet but cheerin welcome. Few, if onny, men ov his day devoted as mich labor an' time to gatherin an' preservin Yorksher literature, to which he wor noa mean contributor. An' another at aw oft met in his company. Grand old Ben Preston,—who has made Gilstead moor a shrine whear pilgrims pay homage to ther native twang. " Natterin' Nan," " Old Moxy," " Th' poor Wayver" an' duzzens sichlike, stampt him *The* Yorkshire poet of his day. Monny moor aw remember, but awm foorsed to skip noatice on 'em;—some have sung ther last sweet strains, an' some are battlin hard to fill th' empty niches death has left.

Peter had a gooid nooas an' he pointed it towards th' Ross Hotel, an' as we all foller'd his leead we wor sooin set anent four pint pots filled wi' what's kept moor teetotal lecturers aght o' th' bastile nor owt else.

We didn't stop long for we'd decided to walk on th' canal bank as far as Bingley, whear Peter sed we could catch another Fly booat at wod tak us on to Skipton withaat a stop.

Aw believe thers thaasands o' folk at live within an' haar's ride o' Saltaire who have noa idea what beauties are spread aght o' ivveryside, an' wod reward 'em, far moor nor a trip to Morecambe or Blackpool, if they'd pay 'em a visit. Aw think aw shall nivver forget that two mile walk to Bingley.

Th' canal banks wor like a carpet o' breet colors—an' th' river ran below,—shaded wi' trees under which th' ground seemed covered wi' a claad ov hyacinths. Th' sweetest scents wor wafted throo ivvery side,—May blossoms wor soa thick on some o'th' thorn trees wol they lukt as if they'd been in a snow storm. Rolling hills stretched far away on awther side, covered wi' ivvery shade ov green, dotted here an' thear wi' cottages 'at seemed th' picturs ov content. We sat daan to admire an' drink it all in an' for th' furst time sin leeavin hooam aw felt thankful at awd come. It just suited me, an' browt to mi mind a song aw used to sing befoor mi voice had crackt an' aw tried to sing it agean.

  Years have passed, but still the time
    Seems as yesterday to me,
  When I held her hand in mine,
    As we sat beneath the tree.
  Then we spake of Trust and Love,—
    Love that was but newly born;
  As we sauntered through the grove,
    When the May hung on the Thorn.

  Fragrance floated on the air,
    And the river sparkled bright,
  Birds were flitting here and there
    Singing to their heart's delight.
  But no bird or flower so sweet
    Ever woke to greet the morn,

As that maid I chanced to meet,
    When the May hung on the Thorn.

Happy days! too quickly spent,—
    Nevermore to dawn for me;—
Soon our Fancy's web was rent
    By a cruel Fate's decree.
Yet I dream the dream again,
    As I wander on forlorn,
And each Fear renews the pain,
    When the May hangs on the Thorn.

Fairy feet still lightly rove
    Mid the blossoms of the Spring;
Bright eyes sparkle in the grove,
    And the birds as sweetly sing.
But their charms no joys impart,
    And my heart must ever mourn,
For the maid who won my heart,
    When the May hung on the Thorn.

"What age wod shoo be when that happened?" sed Crammer.

"What happened?"

"When shoo hung hersen."

"Who does ta meean? Aw think tha doesn't know what tha'rt tawkin abaat."

"Aw meean May, ov coorse. Did'nt ta say 'at shoo hung hersen on a thorn?"

"Aw think tha wants to rooit some o'th' wax aght o' thi ears befoor tha hears another song."

"Tak noa nooatice on him," sed Peter, "it wor a varry nice song an' varry weel sung. Ther's monny a chap at's stooan deeaf 'at wod be fain to hear thi sing that. But let's travel for aw should like to have a bit o' time to spend at Bingley."

We set off agean, an' ivvery step o' th' rooad wor temptin enuff to inspire a poet, but ther's noa moor poetry in a booatman nor ther is in a booat-horse. Sammy didn't feel like tawkin mich for he wor rayther nettled, for a chap likes to feel at he's appreciated even when he's amang fooils. A chap may be in a varry humble position an' still have some noble ideas, but to expect ignoramuses to admire what they cannot understand is as big a mistak as to expect a blind man to admire a beautiful pictur. Longfellow spaiks trewth when he says—

> "When e'er a noble deed is wrought,
> When e'er is spoken a noble thought,
> Our hearts in glad surprise,
> To higher levels rise.
> The tidal wave of deeper souls
> Into our inmost being rolls,
> And lifts us unawares
> Out of all meaner cares."

But th' noblest thowts at Longfellow put into verse could nivver lift chaps like Crammer or Throstle.

Sammywell knew this an' made a resolution at for th' remainder o'th' trip he'd cast noa moor ov his pearls befoor sich swine, an' if th' swine had known, noa daat they'd ha been varry mich obliged to him for havin soa mich consideration.

Bingley wor raiched at last, but that's for another chapter.

## CHAPTER SEVENTH.

### BINGLEY BEAUTIES.

BINGLEY has long been known as "The Throstle Nest of old England," an' noa moor fittin title could be given to it. One of its poets has proudly sung:—

"We have the mountain breeze, the pure cold spring,
 The woods where every British bird doth sing;
 Wild plants and flowers, wild birds, and scenes as
  wild,
 Or soft as any on which Nature smiled.
 For all that generous Nature can bestow,
 All Yorkshire scenes to Bingley vale must bow."

An' as Sammywell lukt raand abaat him, findin beauties ivvery whear, he couldn't resist th' temptation ov tryin his fist at a bit ov rhyme hissen.

Sweet Throstle Nest of England,
 Where Spring first ope's her eye,
Where Summer loves to linger,
 And Autumn grieves to die.

Where Winter's softest snowspread
  Protects the sleeping bloom,
From every rude vicissitude,
  That passes o'er its tomb.
Who does not love thy meadows,
  Thy hills and bosky dells,
Thy woods,—thy sparkling river,
  Thy soul-solacing bells?
Thy grand old church surrounded
  With its illustrious dead,
Thy homes where honest labor
  Can rest its weary head?
Thy patriarchal dwellers
  With locks of silvery white,
Hanging about their ruddy cheeks,
  Which health still renders bright.
Thy sturdy youths and maidens,
  With strength and beauty blest;
All vie to court our praises,—
  Old England's Throstle Nest!

"It's all varry nice, Sammywell," sed Peter, when he'd read it aght to him, "but awr Throstle isn't likely to mak his nest i' Bingley; but as we shall'nt be able to leave here till afternooin, if tha'll point aght a place whear he can peark a bit aw've noa daat that'll suit him. An' tha mun be sewer to pick on a place whear ther's some weet stirrin, for he's net unlike a stormcock,—he sings th' best when he's getten moist.

"Aw think its abaat time at Sammywell did

stand treat," sed Crammer, as he coom up. "Aw've been huggin this spy glass for th' last haar an' moor, an' aw think its abaat time it had a ticket teed on it, an' wor sent back unless he'll let me fix it up soas it'll be ov some use, for its nobbut a lump o' lumber as it is."

"If tha thinks tha can fix it soas it'll be onny gooid, do soa," sed Sammy, for he'd begun to think at th' five shillin it had cost mud ha been put to a better use.

"We'll just call in here," sed Sammy, as he stopt at a public haase at wor just opposite th' church gates, "an' we'll order a bite o' dinner gettin ready, an' then we can have a bit ov a luk raand wol they fix things. Nah yo three can caar aghtside wol aw give th' order."

"Nooan soa," sed Peter, "aw'st want to have a share i' orderin too."

"An' awm sewer yo'll mak a mullock on it if Crammer an' me dooant help yo a bit," sed Throstle.

Soa all four went in an' sat daan in a little raam, an' varry sooin a nice young lass coom to see what they wanted.

"We want a bit o' dinner if yo can let us have it in abaat hawf an haar?" sed Sammy.

"Well," shoo sed, "yo're rayther lat for we've just getten awrs."

"It isn't yors 'at we coom after," sed Peter,

"we want dinners for ussen,—we're nooan particlar what it is if yo give us plenty on it. But furst ov all yo'd better fotch in hawf a gallon o' best ale for us to be gooin on wi'"

"Willn't common do? yo see we'd soa monny visitors coom o' Sundy wol they supt all th' best ale we had, but if common 'll do aw dar say aw can let yo have hawf a gallon; but th' brewer willn't be here befoor to-morn an' we like to keep a sup for us reglar customers."

"Common will do," sed Throstle, an' off shoo went an' wornt long befoor shoo wor back agean. "Yo see," shoo sed, "we'd sich a haase full o' folk o' Sundy wol they ommost ait us aght o'th' hoil, an' as awm here all bi misen aw connot goa aght to buy owt, soa unless yo can mak do wi' some cold rooast beef, or cold boil'd pooark, or some ham an' eggs an' apple pie an' cheese, aw connot sarve yo to-day. But if yo like pickled cabbage or oonions we've lots o' them, an' aw'll have yo a pan full o' puttates boiled in a two-o'-three minnets."

"Stop mistress, if yo pleeas!" sed Crammer; "yo've made my maath watter wol aw connot sup."

"Yo couldn't suit us better, lass," sed Throstle. "Put on th' rooast beef an' th' pooark an' th' pickles, an' a cake or two o' havver breead,—aw see yo've plenty on th' breead flaik, an' let's have lots o' taties, an' yo'll see we'st be able to mak a dinner."

"An' nah," sed Sammywell, "awm baan to have a luk raand wol its ready. Who'll goa wi' me?"

Peter an' Throstle wor willin, but Crammer sed he wor soa tired 'at he thowt he'd rayther sit a bit, soa they went baght him.

Th' furst ov all they went into th' church yard an' lukt at th' gravestooans, an' Sammy wor mich takken up wi' readin 'em, but they didn't interest his companions mich, for Peter sed it nivver wor wise to judge ov a chap's past character bi what fowk put on his gravestooan. But they wor all famously suited wi' th' grand old church, an' th' chap 'at wor i' charge wor varry ready to tell 'em all he knew abaat it. Its been th' witness ov wonderful changes, an' has history sich as few even ov th' oldest can booast. Then Peter led th' way to th' famous canal locks, which are a sample ov what engineerin skill can do. Th' idea ov ivver bein able to tak one o' them big, weighty barges, containin hundreds o' tons ov cargo ovver a hill top must have seemed next to impossible, but they do it daily an' seem to think nowt abaat it; but even i' this day ov ship canals, it stands aght as a wonderful victory ov mind ovver matter. It wod pay onnybody 'at's a taste for marvellous achievements to visit it. Peter wor in his element when he wor describin it, an' Sammy wor capt to find 'at he worn't sich a fooil as he'd takken him to be. He mightn't know mich abaat books, but he could give him some pointers when it coom to booats. Next they paid a visit to th' cemetary, one 'at has few equals awther i' Yorksher or aght on it. Ivvery thing possible seems to have been done to mak it a beautiful restin place. Trees an' flaars are luxuriantly growin on all sides, liftin up one's thowts to things purer, an' fillin one with a desire to be worthier ov the blessins here an' hopeful ov what are promised hereafter. Then a visit had to be paid to th' Park, but th' thowts ov dinner drew 'em back, for they hadn't faith enuff i' Crammer's self denial to think he'd wait for them, an' they feeard th' consequences ov him havin th' furst start.

Luckily they wor just i' time, but they couldn't understand ha it wor at Crammer wor smilin all over his face (what face he had,) an' pairt way daan his neck, an' a steeamin glass o' gin an' watter i'th' front on him, for they knew he hadn't a penny.

"Has this chap been chawkin up?" axd Peter.

"Nay, indeed he nawther!" shoo sed, an' her an' Crammer winkt at one another in a way 'at flammergasted 'em. But they wor too eager to start on th' spreead 'at wor befoor 'em, to waste time on Crammer just then.

They wor all i' fine fettle, an' th' beef wor as tender as a chicken, an' th' pooark fairly melted i' ther maaths. Shoo browt th' pickled cabbage on in a bowl ommost as big as a bucket, an' they dived ther forks into it as if they wor hay makkin, an' fairly worried at it. Th' young mistress had drawn some moor ale an' as fast as a glass showed signs o' bein empty shoo filled it up. "Nah, mak a gooid dinner," shoo sed, "it's net just as nice as aw could ha liked, but it's best we have."

Th' way it disappeared wor its own recommend- ation, an' one after another had to put daan his knife an' fork,—all but Cammer, an' he kept it up wol Sammywell ordered th' lass to tak it away if shoo didn't want to see him chooak.

Nubdy seemed inclined to leeav just then, soa they lit ther bacca an' wor enjoyin a sleepy smook when Crammer rang th' bell.

"Bring us four threepenoths o' Scotch, warm wi' sewgar," he sed, an' shoo went to fotch 'em, wol Sammy an' Peter stared at him as if he'd ordered a case o' shampane an' a box o' cigars.

"Who's baan to pay for 'em, thinks ta?" sed Sammy.

They wor browt in an' Crammer winkt an' sed,

"That'll be all reight," an' shoo sed "thankyo sir," an' winkt back at him.

This wor moor nor Sammy could stand, soa he sed. "Here, young woman,— aw want an explanation o' this! Awm th' paymaister! just tell me what aw owe?"

"Why," shoo sed, "yo had hawf a gallon o' ale, that's eightpence, an' th' dinner's a shillin a piece, an' th' pickled cabbage is fourpence extra, —that's just five shillin."

Sammy threw daan two hawf craans, "Nah then, what aw want to know is who's gooin to pay for th' whisky."

"Oh, nivver mind that. That's a private arrangement between that gentleman an' me."

"The degger it is!" sed Sammy, an' he sank into his seeat wi' a soss, an' he couldn't tak his een off Crammer.

Tothers wor just as fast what to mak on it, an' nubdy spaik for a bit. At last Peter put daan his pipe an' lukkin as fierce as he could, he sed to Crammer, "If awd to knock th' top o' thy heead off tha'd be capt aw reckon?"

"Aw reckon aw should," sed Crammer, turnin varry white, for he wor feeared o' Peter.

"Well, that's just what awm baan to do if tha doesn't explain th' meeanin o' this. Has ta been robbin somdy or has ta been makkin a fooil o' that lass wol we've been aght? Nah, spaik trewth, for tha knows tha connot cram us!"

"Nah, dooant get mad, it's all reight, an' if yo'll let me aw'll tell yo all abaat it."

"Tha'd better," sed Peter, showin him his fist.

"Well, when yo went aght, yond lass coom in to side up, an' shoo saw this spyglass o' Sammy's an' wanted to know what it wor; an' aw sed it wor a new fashioned machine for takkin likeneses, an' shoo sed shoo'd been wantin to have hers takken for a long while, but shoo's nivver able to get aght, soa aw sed if shoo'd gie me th' job awd do it cheeap, an' shoo agreed to gie me eighteenpence, soa aw tuk her into th' backyard, an' pooled it aght as far as it ud come an' tell'd her to luk steady at th' small end, then aw shut it up wi' a bang an' tell'd her it wod be all reight, an' promised to bring it wi' me when aw coom agean. Then aw gate threepenoth o' gin, an' nah we've getten a shillins worth o' whisky, an' aw've another threepenoth to come in."

"Tha'rt a swindler, an' nowt else. They did reight to call thee Crammer!" sed Sammy, "awm hawf inclined to gie thi i' charge."

"Well, yo tell'd me to mak use on it if aw could, an' that's all aw've been able to do up to nah."

Peter went aght an' browt th' lass back wi' him, an' expooased Crammer to his face, an' then he paid for what they'd had, an' warned her to be moor careful i'th' futer.

"Nah aw mun leeav yo for a bit," he sed, " for aw've some enquirements to mak here abaat that carpet bag, an' aw want to know when ther's a Fly booat expected up. Crammer tha'll ha to come wi' me, for tha artn't to be trusted."

"Then Throstle an' me 'll have a walk as far as th' Druid's Alter, its little moor nor a mile, an' we can be back i' plenty o' time."

Havin agreed to meet at th' same place agean, they each went ther own way.

Its a pratty stiff climb up to th' Druid's Alter on a warm day, but thers grand views when yo get thear, an' ther's generally a nice bit o' breeze stirrin. Its just a lot o' big rocks, one especially soa, an' that's what has getten th' name. It's a big square mass, wi' a flat top. Its sed to be 660 feet aboon seah level, an' i' olden times wor used bi th' ancient Druids for religious purposes, an' although its hundreds o' years sin, Bingley wor a place ov importance even then. It wor a treeat to sit thear an' rest a bit an' luk ovver miles an' miles ov glorious country, whear ivverything seemed peaceful an' prosperous. Throstle enjoyed it too, tho' he didn't say mich, but he warbled, in a voice a deal sweeter nor aw believed he had, "Give me a cot in the valley I love," an' then he sighed, an' aw fancied he wor wishin at it had been his lot to be comfortably sattled i' one o' th' little cots at he saw at his feet. It wor sweet to sit an' dream sich things, tho' daatless, could we have seen into some on 'em we should have faand they contained ther full share ov cares an' troubles. Sickness or poverty are hard to bide, but when they booath come at once, ther's noa wonder if a waik mortal sinks under it.

Th' walk back wor easier, an' havin still some time to spare we walked throo th' taan, admirin th' shop winders an' th' new buildins at are been put up—an' th' old market cross, an' th' quaint cottages. Then we fan us way back to th' same place whear we'd been soa weel sarved an' kindly treated, an' wor welcomed wi' a smile at wor worth gooin a mile to see.

We wor sooin after joined bi Peter,—he'd left Crammer daan bi th' canal to wait for us,—an' after a short rest an' a chat, we bid gooid bye, to th' bonniest lass an' th' pleasantest hostess we'd met sin we started off. If ivver aw should visit Bingley agean aw shall call at th' cosy little pub at ovverluks th' church yard.

We wor sooin at th' canal,—th' booat wor ready,—we stept on booard, an' left wi' leetsome hearts, one o' th' sweetest nooks i' Yorkshire.

F

## CHAPTER EIGHTH.

#### FUN ON A FLY BOOAT.

SAMMYWELL wor sittin quietly watchin th' objects as they seemed to be glidin past, when Throstle coom an' sat daan beside him, an' after beggin a match, an' leetin his pipe, he sed, "Have yo seen Crammer sin we started off?"

"Aw've nawther seen him nor want to see him," sed Sammywell.

"Aw nobbut thowt yo'd like to see ha he's fixed th' spy glass. It seems to work varry weel nah. He's a bit ov a genius in his way. He'd ha made a gooid tinker if he'd been eddicated."

"Awd better be havin a luk at it then," sed Sammywell, an' off he went to Crammer who wor at tother end o'th' booat.

"Soa tha's managed to fix it up has ta?" he sed as he drew up to him.

"Eeah, aw think it'll be ov a bit o' use nah."

"But what are ta dooin wi' it stuck i' that

bucket o' watter? Doesn't ta know tha'll tak th' polish off it?"

"Ne'er heed th' polish! Just yo watch it work," an' he seized how'd on it bi th' eyepiece an' pooled it aght as far as it wod come, an' then he lifted it up an' squirted aght abaat a gallon o' watter.

"Why, tha gurt leatherheead!" sed Sammy, "tha's ruined it!"

"Aw dooant know ha yo can mak that aght. Aw've made a poor spy glass into a gooid squirter an' aw think yo owt to be satisfied. Monny a chap's gien me a shillin for dooin less nor that. It wants nowt but a rayther bigger sucker puttin in an' then it'll do for swillin th' winders or owt like that."

"Then tha'd better put thisen in! When Mally sees that shoo'll have summat to say."

After all he hadn't made sich a bad job on it considerin, for he'd fixed a piece o' tin at wor full o' hoils,—like th' nozzle ov a watterin can, onto th' end on it, an' it did its wark fairly weel, an' when Peter an' Throstle brast aght laffin, Sammy couldn't help but join in.

"Tha'll have to hug it nah wol we get to Liverpool," sed Sammy, "an' nah, Peter, ha are we gettin on, an' which is th' next stoppin place, an' what time does th' laance come raand? Tha mun stick to thi bargain tha knows, an' its thee at has to find th' grub, etsetterer."

"Well, tha sees, Sammy, bein as we're all officers, we're net expected to want owt between meals, soa tha mun be as patient as tha can wol to-morn at braikfast time, an' then we'st be at Keighley."

"O, that's it is it? An' then when we get to Keighley it'll be my turn to pay agean! That isn't gooid enuff for Sammywell! It's nowt but a shuffle to get off payin thi wack! Aw'll tell awr Mally what sooart ov a cussin shoo's getten. Aw dooant see ha tha maks it aght 'at we're all officers, soa long as we've nowt to do!"

"That's just it. Th' moor yo are an officer an' th' less yo have to do. Aw thowt tha knew that. Tha sees tha'rt commodore an 'awm th' captain, an' Throstle's a mate o' mine, an' as aw knew him befoor Crammer, he's th' furst mate, an Crammer's second mate. Nah, does ta see ha it is?"

"Noa, aw dunnot! an' aw dooant meean to see ha it is unless tha finds us summat to ait an' drink! Tha'll nawther ha me for a commodoor nor a troopadoor at that price. Aw'll get Throstle an' Crammer onto my side an' start a mutiny, an' if we dooant pitch thee ovverbooard,—as big as tha art,—tha may be thankful!"

"Sammywell!" shaated Throstle, "yo're wanted."

"Awm commin!" an' off he sat, in a fewmin rage, cloisly foller'd bi Peter.

"Cant ta smell summat?" sed Throstle.

"Eeah! Aw can smell ther's some trubble brewin for somdy if they dooant alter! They'd better net put on me too far, for awm a dangerous man when mi monkey's up!"

"Tha'll find Crammer daan i'th' cabin, an' th' captain's just gooan daan, an' tha'll have summat to wrastle wi' daan thear. Awm commin too."

"Ther's summat 'at smells varry nice, schews what it is," sed Sammy, sniftin. "If ther's onny wrastlin o' that sooart gooin on, awm in at it!" an' he ommost tummeld daan th' steps, foller'd bi Throstle. Peter wor laffin wol he made th' booat shake, an' Crammer wor grinnin wol yo could caant all his double teeth, an' if th' hinge at th' back ov his neck had given way he'd ha lost th' top ov his heead.

Ther wor varry little raam, but ther wor a table wi' a big tin full o' ham steaks on a table, an' two looaves o' breead, an' on th' floor, cloise to Peter, wor a box wi' two duzzen bottles wi' red labels on em.

"Aw suppooas tha thinks tha's been havin me on a bit, Peter, but tha'rt mistaen. Aw knew all th' time 'at tha wor nubbut tryin to get me shirted, but aw know a trick worth two o' that.

Aw know tha doesn't keep up that corporation on th' honor ov bein a officer."

"Well, start on, an' be sewer tha doesn't tell Mally owt abaat it."

"Tha'rt a trump, Peter! an' aw allus sed soa. Awm sooary for thy sake 'at Mally hadn't a sister. Tha mightn't ha made as gooid a husband as me, but tha'd ha been a fair average aw believe. Which officer's duty is it to draw them corks?"

"Ivverybody for thersen, but th' captain furst," sed Peter, seizin hold o'th' corkscrew.

Ther wor nubdy to interfere wi' 'em, an' as they wor all bent on enjoyin thersen, they made a merry little party.

"Tawkin abaat officers," sed Crammer, wipin whear his chin owt to be, wi' th' back ov his hand, "reminds me ov a bit ov a trick 'at wor played on a poleece officer at Idle. Yo happen nivver knew Jooany Kellet? well, he wor a dry sooart ov a customer——"

"Net mich like thee, then," sed Sammy.

"An' he wor varry fond ov a jooak, an' he wor noa favorite wi' th' poleece on that accaant. Fowk 'at live i' Idle seem mooastly to be varry fond o' dogs, but net varry fond o' payin th' license, an' as ther'd been some complaints, one o'th' poleece, a young chap 'at fancied hissen a gooid bit, wor towld off, to goa abaat i' plain clooas an' find aght who wor evadin th' law.

One neet he called in at th' Dumb Bell an' ordered a drink. Ther wor a nice company an' Kellett wor amang 'em. Th' poleeceman thowt 'at nubdy knew him, but Jooany spotted him as sooin as he coom in, an' in a bit he managed to turn th' tawk onto dogs. "Why, tha hasn't a dog, has ta Jooanas?" axt one.

"Eeah, aw've kept a dog for monny a year."

"Why, aw've nivver seen it. Does ta pay a license for it?"

"Noa, aw nivver pay noa license, why should aw? It's nivver aght o'th' haase an' mels o' nubdy," sed Jooany.

"Tha'll get dropt on somday if tha doesn't mind."

"Nay, net aw! They'll want some sharper poleece nor they've getten befoor they can drop o' me."

Th' poleeceman chuckled to hissen, an' supt up, an' off he went to Kelletts. He knockt at th' door, an' when Mistress Kellett oppened it, he sed, "Is th' maister in?"

"Nay, he isn't, but awm expectin him; will yo walk in an' wait a bit?"

"Eeah, aw dooant mind if aw do," he sed, an' when he gate in he lukt all raand, but he could see noa dog.

"Dooant yo find it looansum livin here, when

Jooany's away? aw should ha thowt yo'd ha kept a dog in a place like this."

"We have a dog, but it's moor for ornament nor use."

"Is that soa?" he sed. "Aw should like to see it. Awm a gurt admirer o' dogs. Have yo a license for it?"

"Nay, net we marry! yo can come into th' paylor an luk at it if yo like," an' shoo tuk th' cannel an' led th' way. "Here it is," shoo sed, pointin to a glass case whear a little stuffed dog wor standin, lukkin as natteral as life. "It's a beauty, isn't it?"

"It is. Did he stuff it hissen?"

"Eeah, he's allus made a hobby o' stuffin stuff."

"Well, aw willn't wait onny longer," he sed, "or he'll happen be stuffin me."

When he gate aghtside ther wor a crack o' laffin, for Jooany had let all th' chaps into th' saycret, an' he felt like pailin his heead ageean a wall. Net sich a bad trick wor it."

"Well, after that," sed Peter, "aw think Throstle should give us a bit ov a ditty."

Throstle nivver wanted axin twice, an' he struck up,

> This world is very funny,
> For no matter how much money
> Man is earning, he will spend it,
>     And be hard up all the time;

To his utmost he is straining,
To catch up without attaining,
Till he makes his life a burden,
    When it should be bliss sublime.

He who earns a thousand, merely,
Thinks about two thousand yearly
Would be just the proper figure
    To make happiness complete;
But his income when it doubles,
Only multiplies his troubles,
For his outgo then increases,
    Making both ends worse to meet.

It is run in debt and borrow,
Flush to-day and broke to-morrow,
Scheming, planning, every way,
    To put off the day of doom;
Spending money e'er he makes it,
And then wondering what takes it,
Till he, giving up the riddle,
    Looks for rest within the tomb.

Yes, this world is very funny,
Man is always after money,
Tho' the happiness it promises
    Is ne'er within his touch;
When he's dead, relations quarrel,
And although he left a barrel,
They are every one dissatisfied,
    That it wasn't twice as much.

"Let Throstle sup," sed Sammywell. "Awm

sewer he desarves it. Ha are th' bottles gettin on, Captain?"

"Ther's two or three left get."

"Aw'll tell thi what awm thinkin. Tha made a mistak when tha sed we should mak a nice quart ette,—aw think a gallon ette wod be nearer th' messer. But ther's noa wonder when Crammer's amang us. Aw've a nooation 'at if Nooah had had one or two like him i'th' ark some on 'em wod ha had to goa short befoor th' forty days wor up. But if yo'll excuse me, aw'll goa up on top an' have a breeath o' fresh air, an' then awst be able to sleep a bit happen."

It wor a glorious neet. Th' mooin wor like a silver shield in a pale blue sky, an' net a claad to be seen. It reminded Sammywell ov William Dearden, another Yorksher poet, who has gone to a better land; an' th' openin lines ov his "Star Seer" coom to Sammywell's lips,—

"Who loves not night,—when through the violet hued
  O er arching heavens, the starry multitude,
  As through a shining curtain smiling peep,
  Like angel's eyes,—watching a world asleep?"

All wor silent, except for th' rumble an' splash at th' screw made in awr wake. Net a solitary bird chirped, nor a footstep could be heard. Net even a saunterin pair ov lovers could be seen, an' th' trees wor as motionless as if they wor carved aght o' rock. Two men were curled up asleep, an' one stood wi' th' tiller in his hand guidin us on, silently, as if afeeard ov disturbin a sleepin land. Th' hills wor partly hid, as if Nature had thrown a robe o' mist ovver 'em, to shield 'em lest even th' mooin's rays should mar ther rest.

Sammywell sat long an' when at last he went to th' little bunk 'at he knew Peter's forethowt wod have provided, he walkt o' tippy tooa, for fear at th' saand ov his footfall should jar th' silence 'at seemed to reign everywhear.

He faand his friends all fast asleep, an' he crept quietly into th' corner at wor waitin for him. Weary wi' his day's tramp, an' wi' a mind at peeace wi' all th' world,—gratefully he curled hissen up, an' as sleep laid her heavy hand on him he muttered—" Keep thi own side, Mally lass, an' dooant thrust soa."

For haars he slept on, an' ha long he mud ha done it isn't to tell, but th' tramplin aboon his heead, an' th' saand o' men's voices made him start up to find he wor alooan.

Peter met him wi' a cheery " Gooid mornin," an' after he'd had a swill wi' clean cold watter he felt as breet as a bee.

Th' mornin wor as grand as onnybody could wish, an' he wor ready for off at once, but Peter advised him to wait abit, an' he wor quite willin to do soa, for ivverything wor bustle an' all wor new to him. Ther wor booats ov different kinds, layin cloise together, an' he could step off one to th' tother, an' altho he wor stared at a gooid deeal it didn't prevent him shovin his nooas whearivver he fancied ther wor owt to be seen. His opinion o'th' class o' men at managed an' labored amang sich strange unwieldy craft began to change, for altho' rough lukkin i' some cases, th' mooast on 'em wor quite a superior class ov workin men.

When he gat back to his own booat, as he rayther praadly called it, Peter signaled him to join 'em, an' he wor sooin enjoyin some hot coffee, th' best he thowt he'd ivver tasted in his life, an' breead like biscuit, wi' butter sweet an nutty, an' a big bunch o' fresh spring oonions, an' lettuce 'at seemed to taste o'th' dew drops.

"When aw get hooam agean, awm baan to have my coffee made in a tin can, it tastes better bi th' hawf. Aw wonder whear aw could buy some coffee th' same quality as this?" inquired Sammy.

"Why this coffee wor bowt i' Leeds, an' aw dar say yo're Mally will sit daan to some just as gooid, an' maybe better. It's nooan th' difference i'th' coffee, it's th' difference 'at's takkin place i' thisen," sed Peter. "But nah it's time we wor gettin off, for aw see they're preparin for gooin. Let's see if we can find this carpet bag at Keighley."

## CHAPTER NINTH.

#### PUTTIN' ON STYLE.

THO' it isn't possible to admire Keighley for its beauty, yet ther's plenty to interest one, an' it's soa situated, at whichivver way yo goa when leavin it, they all lead to places beautiful, romantic or celebrated. Onnybody can see at Keighley wor nivver planned. Its been thrown together, higgle-ti-pigglety, as it chonced to suit times, circumstances, or convenience. It has some gooid buildings, if yor lucky enuff to find 'em, yo'll admit,—plenty ov handsome shops,—a fair sprinklin ov factories an' workshops,—here an' thear some quaint dwellins ov ancient date,—an' on all sides, new cottages, an' what may be called middle class haases, at its to be hooaped mak up i' comfortable insides, for th' want ov beauty aghtside. But its a place for business, yo can't help nooaticin that. Gettin hold o' some 'brass,' seems to be ivverybody's object for five days an' a hawf i' ivvery wick, an' th' Setterdy afternooin is set apart for seein whear they can mak ther markets to th' best advantage; an' Sunday, to rest an' religion. Ther's noa raam i' Keighley for fowk at's too idle to work. They have a varry nice park whear they can goa if they should ivver have time. But Keighley fowk are nooated for industry, honesty, an' hospitality. Ther's nowt meean abaat 'em. A visitor is allus welcome to th' best at th' haase affoords. Th' men are hearty an' intelligent, an' th' wimmen are moor sowt after for wives nor onny other, unless it be Haworth lasses. (Sammywell gate his wife throo Haworth.)

Peter an' his two mates went to mak some enquiries abaat th' lost carpet bag, leeavin' Sammywell to spend his time as best suited him, promisin to meet him in an' haar's time at th' Baancin Besom. After sich a gooid braikfast as he had just had, he didn't feel inclined for onny refreshment just then, soa he thowt he'd tak a walk raand an' see what alterations had been made sin he wor last thear, hooapin to meet wi' some friends who had treated him weel on former visits. He hadn't gooan far befoor he saw hissen in a big lukkin glass at wor in a shop winder.

"Bi gow!" he sed, "but that can nivver be me! Aw nivver saw misen luk sich a seet i' all mi life! Aw darn't goa onny farther for fear aw'st be lockt up! Whativver wor awr Mally thinkin on to turn me aght sich a scarecrow as this! Here have aw been fancyin 'at ivverybody wor smilin becoss they wor fain to see me, an they've nobbut been grinnin to see what a fooil aw lukt. But aw'll sooin alter this."

Soa he set off to find a clooas shop, an' as it happened he hadn't far to goa.

"Aw want a new rig aght, maister," he sed to th' shopkeeper.

"Aw hardly think we've getten owt i' yor line," sed th' chap, "for yo see we dooant do onny business wi' show actors, nor buskers. Yo'd be moor likely to pick up summat to suit yo at a pop shop."

"Dooant thee mak onny mistak, lad. Aw want a daycent suit for a daycent chap at a daycent price, an' aw dooant want it on tick nawther, soa tha can get agate if tha's onny to sell."

"Certainly," sed th' chap, quite respectful like. "Ha do you think summat i' this line ud suit yo?" an' he showed him a nice dark blue suit, at wor on a figure at th' door.

"What's th' price?" sed Sammy, feelin at th' quality.

"Well, seein at yor th' furst customer to-day aw'll let yo have it for fifty shillin, but it should be two paand ten."

"Tha does reight to favor me a bit, lad,—just let's try it on."

"If it fits one dummy it should fit another," sed th' chap, spaikin low daan to hissen; but Sammy heeard him, an' if it hadn't ha been 'at he couldn't fashion to be seen aght i' what he had on he'd ha left it; but as it wor he tried 'em on an' they fit him as if they'd been made on his back. Th' chap didn't sell hats but he went aght an' gate one for him, a stove pipe,— 'at shone like silk, which in fact it wor; an' when he lukt at hissen he sed,—

"Gimminy! Sammy! Tha wants nowt nah but a clean dicky an' thi shoes polishin to mak onnybody mistak thi for a gentleman."

He paid his bill, an' wor gooin aght when th' chap called him back to know whear he'd to send his old clooas to.

"Send 'em to ——, noa, tha'd better net. Mak 'em into a bundle an' send 'em to Mistress Mally Grimes at Bradforth."

"All right, sur, an' thank yo," sed th' chap, an' Mister Grimes stept aght an' walked up th' street wi' as mich style abaat him as if he'd come to buy th' Mechanics Hall. He wor passin a barber's shop whear it wor painted on th' winder, "Shaving one penny."

"Awm spendin brass at a famous rate," he sed, "but its a pity to spoil a ship for th' sake ov a penotn o' tar," soa he went in an' had a shave an' put daan a penny.

"Another penny, sir, if yo pleeas," sed th' barber.

"Ha's that? Yo're sign says 'shavin *one* penny.'"

"Yes, sir, but we allus charge double price for a double chin."

"All reight, but it's a barberous custom, but aw'll get even wi' thi, for aw'll bring Crammer at hasn't onny chin soa tha'll ha to shave him for nowt."

In another shop he bowt a collar an' a umberel, an' he railly did luk a varry respectable old codger.

"Nah, its abaat time aw went to th' Baancin Besom," he sed, an' as he'd oft been thear i' former times he'd noa trubble i' findin it. As he wor gooin into th' tap raam th' mistress called aght—

"This way, sir,—this way to the bar parlour!"

"What a difference a suit o' clooas maks," he sed, as he set daan in a cushioned cheer, "but aw expect aw'st have to pay extra." He called for a small sherry an' bitters, an' as he wor drinkin it he heeard Peter an' Throstle an' Crammer goa into th' tap raam.

"He's nooan getten here yet," he heeard 'em say, an' then they knockt on th' table an' ordered a quairt. In a minnit or two at after he heeard Peter tawkin to th' lanlady.

"Has ther been an old chap enquirin for us?" axt Peter.

"Net 'at aw know on," shoo sed, "what sooart ov a chap did yo expect?"

"He's a simple lukkin old chap at's wearin a old strawbengy. Yo'd fancy he wor wrang in his heead bi th' luk on him, but he's reight enuff when yo get to know him. He wed a cussin o' mine."

"Well, he hasn't been here, for ther's nubdy i' th' haase but yorsen an' a middle aged gentleman 'at's i'th' best raam."

"Well, when he comes tell him whear we are if he cannot find us,—an' he is rayther gawmless at times."

"They say listeners nivver hear onny gooid o' thersen," sed Sammy, "but they hear trewth sometimes. But aw'll keep 'em waitin a bit, just to sarve 'em aght for spaikin ther minds soa freely," an' he rang th' bell an' ordered another sherry an' bitters. When shoo browt it in, Sammy sed,—

"Yo've getten some compny i'th' tapraam aw hear."

"Nobbut three rough lukkin chaps, they're nowt i' yo're line,—they're waitin for some sooart ov a hawfwit,—'at one on 'em says wed his cussin, but if his cussin is owt like him he aidn't get mich ov a bargain awm thinkin. Ther's all sooarts o' fowk to put up wi' when yo keep a public haase, but for my pairt awd rayther have ther raam nor ther compny. Yo've noa idea! Nah, ther's some pleasur i' waitin on a gentleman like yo are, becoss yo know manners, but sich as them know nowt but ha to guzzle all th' ale they can get," an' shoo whewed aght quite indignant becoss shoo heeard 'em knockin for another quairt.

Sammy wor soa suited wol he called for a cigar, an' kept her soa long wol he wor pickin one, at they knockt agean soa hard at it wor a wonder th' pitcher didn't smash. Then shoo went to 'em.

"Connot yo have a bit o' patience," shoo sed, "aw connot run away all in a minnet when awm waitin on quality fowk!"

"That's all reight, mistress. That old codge. hasn't been yet, has he?"

"Nay, ther's nubdy been as yet."

"It's a queer doo. He sewerly isn't lost."

"Moor likely th' poleece have collared him, for he is a seet whearivver he is. Aw havn't mich i'th' way o' gooid luks to crack on, but aw do luk daycent aside o' him," sed Crammer.

"That's true enuff," sed Throstle, "but then tha sees he's Peter's cussin bi weddin, an' if he's getten into some bother, it may disgrace Peter. An' bi what aw've seen on him, up to nah, he's just one o' them 'at's likely to do it. Aw think we'd better sup up an' mak some enquiries at th' poleece station."

"Why," sed th' mistress, "if he's net altogether thear an' hasn't his reight wits abaat him, he's to be pitied. Awm capt yo'd leeav him, especially in a place like Keighley; for sin it wor made into a taan an' gate a member o' parlyment ov its own it's a dangerous place."

"Well, let's be off," sed Peter, an' as Sammy heeard 'em gooin aght he joined 'em, an' they all went aght together.

"Well, whear are yo for th' next?" sed Sammy when they gate into th' street.

They all stared at him oppen maath. If he'd just dropt aght ov a parryshooit they couldn't ha been moor surprised. Throstle an' Crammer wor feeard to wink lest he should disappear, an' Peter put his hand on him to mak sewer at he wor solid.

"Is this Mister Sammywell Grimes Esquire?" he sed.

"To th' best o' my knowledge that's my cognomen."

"Well, aw'll be blowed!'

"Tha needs noa blowin;—tha'rt full o' wind as it is."

"Tha mun excuse me, Sammy, but tha knows fowk arn't to be blamed for judgin bi appearances, when they've nowt else to goa by, an' aw must say tha lukt like a fooil, tho aw hardly liked to believe tha wor one, an' aw will say, nah, 'at aw see thi donned up, at Mally didn't happen mak sich a mistak after all."

"It's all reight, Peter. If a chap will play at bein a fooil he's noa reight to find fault if fowk tak him for one. But what's th' next move on th' booard for to-day?"

"To start wi', tha mun know at aw've getten onto th' track o' that carpet bag, an' if it isn't at Skipton it's at th' far end, an' we've nowt to do but enjoy ussen wol three o'clock, an' then we catch th' next Fly Booat which will bring us to Skipton to-neet, when we shall goa on a barge at's gooin reight to Bootle. Is ther onny place tha'd like to goa to?"

"Aw should like to walk as far as Haworth,— its nobbut abaat four miles."

"Awm feeard we shalln't have time for that, but ther's a friend o' mine at lives here at knew all th' Bronte family, an' can tell thi moor abaat 'em nor mooast fowk i' Haworth know. He'll be fain to see us, an' if tha likes to goa aw'll gie Throstle a shillin, an' him an' Crammer can goa whear they like wol time for us to start."

"Nowt could suit me better," sed Sammywell,

soa Throstle an' Crammer were sent off an' Peter tuk Sammy to see his old friend Shackleton.

Th' old man wor delighted to see 'em, an' they'd hardly getten set daan befoor ther wor a plentyful supply ov aitables an' drinkables set anent 'em;—it's a way they have at Keighley,—an' after they'd paid ther respects to all th' gooid things they sattled daan for a gossip. He wor a rare specimen ov a Yorksherman at's spent his life amang th' hills whear th' fresh air gives a colour to ther cheeks at old age cannot fade.

He wor full ov stories abaat Carrodus—"Th' grandest fiddler at ivver lived sin Pagganini," he sed, "an' he wor just as clivver twenty year sin as he is to-day, but like th' rest ov geniuses, fowk neglected to honour him as he desarved to be honoured, until th' best part ov his life wor spent, an' his native taan's fowk nobbut acknowledged his wonderful talent after th' rest o' th' world had rewarded it."*

When he gat onto his favorite topic he wor booath enthusiastic an' eloquent; an' it wor a rare treeat to lissen to one who had lived i' daily intercourse wi' a family who shed a lustre ovver Haworth 'at placed it at once among th' shrines whear a world pays homage. "Old Bronte, wor a queer old stick, but a varry fair parson an' a

---

\* Carrodus, the great violinist is since dead.

gooid christian," he sed, "he wor a bit twazzy at times, but one shouldn't judge him harshly, becoss he wor Irish an' couldn't help it. But Charlotte wor my favourite! Shoo wor a nice lass, tho' yo wodn't ha thowt shoo'd as mich in her as shoo had, but 'still watters run deep.' Aw allus think weddin spoilt her. Aw think fowk at write books nivver owt to get wed. A'a, an' what a clivver chap Bramwell wor! If it hadn't been for his gooid nater;—it wor that 'at ruined him. Aw've had monny a glass wi' him at th' Black Bull when his father thowt he wor i' bed. Aw dooant believe he ivver gate onny credit for clivverness, just becoss ov his fondness for drink, but do yo know its my belief at " Wuthering Heights" owed moor to Bramwell nor he wor ivver credited wi' His tother sisters aw nivver made mich on, but awm tell'd they wor clivver, but Charlotte an' Bramwell wor my favorites."

An' mich moor he sed an' wod ha sed, but time wor pressin, an' after thankin him for th' pleasant haar spent in his hospitable cot, Sammy an' Peter bid gooid bye, but net until they'd promised to call agean as sooin as they could.

Soa makkin ther way to th' canal, they faand th' booat ready for off an' Throstle an' Crammer fast asleep.

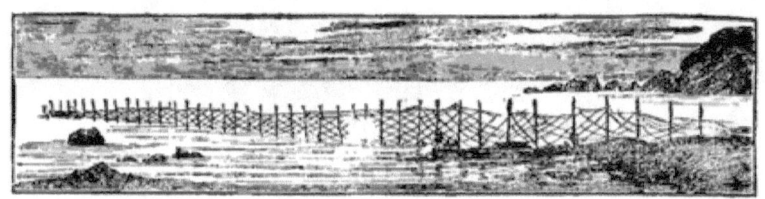

## CHAPTER TENTH.

### SKIPPING OFF TO SKIPTON.

SAMMY wor sooin convinced at th' brass he'd paid for his clooas wor a gooid investment. As sooin as th' booat started off, Peter browt him a box to sit on, an' covered it wi' some seckin for fear his britches should be muckied, an' then he left him wol he went to have a chat wi' a chap Sammy didn't know. Throstle an' Crammer slept on, an' judgin bith luk on 'em, they must have spent ther shillin well if net wisely. But Sammy wor glad to be quiet a bit an' to enjoy th' beauties as they passed. After leeavin dry streets, an' stooans an' mortar, it seemed like enterin on a new world;—a world ov gentle swellin hills, dotted wi' woods i' all ther verdant glory. Hedges sprinkled wi' sweet smellin blossoms,—banks at sparkled wi' dog daises an' butter cups an' wild violets, an' brooad fields, like speckled carpets stretchin for miles, until they seemed to melt away into th' pure blue sky.

"Lives there a man with soul so dead,
Who never to himself has said,
This is my own,—my native land?"

repeated Sammy. "What can onny Yorksherman lang for, moor nor he has at hooam, if he'll nobbut luk for it?" he sed, "an' what charms for lovers ov Nature are within walkin distance ov whear aw am nah. If Craven vale could be carried to Switzerland ther's scoors o' Yorksher fowk wod pay an' travel to see it, an' nivver after grow weary ov tawkin abaat it, but becoss its at ther varry doors they awther dooant believe it exists, or if they do they neglect it. Whear can yo find bonnier villages nor Silsden; Steeton—Kildwick, or Addingham. Bolton Woods are moor visited nor mooast places, but ha few Leeds fowk know owt abaat Malham Cove,—Jennet's Cave,—Gordale Scarr, Malham Tarn or Kilnsey Crag, except what they may sometimes read in a book or a newspaper?" An' occupied wi' recollections ov happy days ov long ago, Sammywell smoked his pipe an' watched th' sun sink lower, an' th' sky tak on a rooasy tint 'at augured weel for another fine day. Th' burds twittered amang th' bushes as they prepared to rest, an' sooin all wor soa quiet wol th' lappin ov th' watter agean th' booat an' th' bank wor all th' saand at fell on his ear. Then

"Straight through the sunset flew a thrush,
 And sang the only song he knew,
Perched on a blooming elder bush;
 (Oh, but to give his song its due!)
  Sang it, and ceased, and left it there
  To haunt bush, blade, and golden air.

Oh, but to make it plain to you!
 (My words were wrought for grosser stuff,)
To give that lovely tune its due
 Never a word is sweet enough;
  A thing to think on when 'twas past,
  As is the first rose or the last."

An' as it piped away Sammy clooased his een, an' dooazin dreamed at Mally wor by his side,—net th' Mally 'at he'd left i' Bradford a day or two sin, but th' rooasy cheeked, shy, modest lass who had wandered wi' him, hand i' hand, when he wor young an' strong, an' all life's lessons wer to leearn. An' then he suddenly wakkened, to find hissen wonderin whether they intended to get th' drinkin ready, for soa mich studdyin gave him a appetite. Throstle an' Crammer had getten up an' wor havin a swill wi' cold watter, net afoor they needed it, an' Peter wor still tawkin to th' strange chap at tother end o' th' booat, soa he shook hissen into shap an' joined 'em.

"This is Skipton at we're just commin to," sed Peter, i' answer to Sammy. "Throstle an' Crammer will have to goa on tother booat at's looadin, an aw shall have to stop wi' this a bit for aw've some business to do, but tha'd better get off an' goa to th' Black Horse,—its easy to find for its cloois to th' church,—an' get what tha wants, an' wait for me."

"All serene," sed Sammywell, an' a few minnits after he wor axin his way to th' Black Horse. On his way thear he had his een abaat him; "Nah, ther's some sense in a taan like this," he sed, "ther's some raam to stir. Ther isn't a street i' Bradford at's as wide as this. Aw could nivver tell th' reason why when fowk start a taan, an' have moor land nor they know what to do wi', they should huddle th' haases all in a lump, wi' nowt but ginnels an' snickets to seperate 'em. They connot even tell which quarter th' winds in unless they can see th' weathercock on th' church steeple, for it gits soa twisted an' twined amang ther back yards an' passages wol it seems to come throo all quarters at once, an' it twirls an' whirls th' dust abaat till it fills yor een an' sifts daan th' back o' yor neck at th' same time. An' th' haases are soa cloice together wol yo mud ommost as weel be all livin i' one, for if yo punce th' foirirons ovver i' yor own kitchen yo'll wakken th' child at's i'th' haase opposite. Awm sewer at if Mally an' me have a bit ov a tiff i' th' afternooin it's sarved up as a relish to th' drinkin i' ivvery haase i'th' fowld when th' husbands comes hooam; an' yo connot rost a bit o' beef withaat th' naybors smellin it an' commin to borrow drippin. Awm glad to see at Skipton fowk have moor sense. This is th' haase awm lukkin for at onnyrate. It's a gooid job aw've changed mi clooas, for they'd ha foired me aght i' quicksticks if awd been wearin tothers. It luks a varry respectable shop, an' aw see they've a rare lump o' beef hung up i' th' passage. If that wor i' Bradford it ud be 'Gooid bye beef,' when they wanted it."

Sammy made his way into th' bar an' called for a glass o' ale, an' wor wonderin whether or net he should order a drinkin or wait wol Peter coom. Wol he wor undecided, a little lad coom in wi' a letter an' axd 'if ther wor onnybody called Sammywell Grimes stoppin thear?"

"That's me," sed Sammy, an' takkin th' lette. he saw it wor throo Peter, to tell him to order beds for 'em booath, an' net to wait for him as he had to see abaat shippin a lot o' goods throo Dewhirst's mill. Th' lanlord had been watchin him rayther suspiciously at furst, but he coom to shake hands wi' him nah.

"And so you are the real, old, original, Sammywell Grimes?" he sed, "I'm pleased to see you. Matilda!" he shaated, an' his wife coom in,—"tell Emma an' Jane an' Eliza to come here quick," an' in a minnet ther wor a flutter o' petticoits an' they all coom in an' wor foller'd bi hawf a duzzen chaps. "This," sed th' lanlord, pointin to me,—" is

> Sammywell Grimes that poor old man,
>   We ne'er shall see him more;
> He used to wear an old brown coat,
>   With buttons down before.

its worth a week's wages to say you've seen him."

"Is that him at had his picter i' th' poleece gazette," ax'd one o'th' chaps.

"No," sed th' lanlord, "he has'nt had it in YET."

"Why, then, who is he?" axt Matilda.

"Have yo never heard of Sammywell Grimes?" axt th' lanlord, but ther worn't one i' all th' lot at ivver had, soa he ordered 'em all back to ther wark an' sed they wor a lot o' hignerent hasses!

Sammywell had a quiet laff all to hissen, an' then he called for another glass, an' axt if him an' Captain Garlick could each be accommodated wi' a bed for th' neet.

That wor sattled satisfactorily, an' just then a big hansum chap coom in an' after starin at Sammy for a while, he set daan cloise to him an' whisperd,—

"Is your name Grimes?"

"It is, sir."

"You're wanted at the ship immediately."

"That's a licker!" sed Sammy, "aw wonder what's up nah? Has Peter brokken his neck or have they let my talescope fall ovverbooard?" he wondered, but he set off at once, an' this chap follered him. "Aw'll bet its summat serious," he thowt, "for aw believe this chap is a detective or summat o' that sooart. It's varry likely awther Throstle or Crammer have getten collard for summat. If its Throstle, aw dooant mind gooin bail for him, but if its Crammer, he can stop i' jail for me, an' sarve him reight for what he sed at Keighley."

"This is th' place," sed th' chap.

"What place?"

"This is th' Ship Hotel whear a gentleman wants to see yo."

"Oh! that's it, is it? Aw thowt yo meant th' ship aw've been sailin in."

Just then th' lanlord coom aght, an' all wor as plain as th' nooas o' mi face.

"Come in, Sammy!" he sed.

"Why, Backerly, ha did yo know aw wor i' Skipton?"

"Captain Garlick's just been in to tell me."

"An' whear is he?"

"He's thrang somewhear, but he'll come as sooin as he can."

This wor a varry lucky meetin for Sammy, for

Backerly an' him had met monny a time befoor. Nowt wod do but Sammy should have his drinkin. A'a! an' what a drinkin! Fresh air may be a varry gooid thing in its way, but they get summat else beside that to live on at Skipton. It wor a spreead fit for a king, an' when Sammy left th' table he couldn't ha pickt a soverin off th' floor if ther'd been one. Then he wor introduced to a lot o' congenial sowls, an' sooin ther wor signs ov a jovial haar. Ther wor songs an' tales an' recitations,—an' gooid ens too,—an Philip,—(that wor him 'at Sammy thowt wor a detective,) recited Shakespeare wol th' gas burned blue. Then Peter turned up, but it wor too lat for him to join in, for it wor shuttin up time, an' soa after biddin 'em all gooid neet, an' promisin to call i'th' mornin, they went to th' Black Horse an' wor sooin i' bed an' asleep.

---

"Aw wonder what they tak us for?" sed Peter as they sat daan to braikfast next mornin. "Just luk at this dish o' ham an' eggs! Ther's enuff to start a restrant."

"Aw'll tell thi what it is," sed Sammy, "they tawk abaat theas country taans beein healthy places to live in, an' they booast abaat ther fresh air an' sichlike, but it's my belief at if fowk whear aw come throo had sich a table to sit daan to as theas fowk have, they'd be healthy too."

Wol they wor dooin ther best to put it aght o'th' seet, Peter explained 'at th' booat he wanted to goa on couldn't get off befoor nooin, an' as they wor shorthanded he wor givin 'em all th' help he could, an' soa Sammy wod have all th' mornin to spend as he thowt fit.

"Aw wish awd bowt this suit a size bigger," sed Sammy, "for if this sooart o' livin goas on long they'll be too little. Aw could do wi' th' buttons shiftin bi nah. If aw wor a single chap aw should like to booard here; for booath bed an' booard an' th' prices suit my taste an' mi pocket."

Peter hurried off, an' Sammy, after havin a bit ov a chat wi' th' young woman at wor sidin th' plates, strolled daan to th' Ship, whear Philip had promised to meet him. He faand him waitin, an' they set aght for a walk.

One o'th' furst things they saw wor a rigiment ov volunteers, an' weel they lukt i' ther scarlet coits. "They're all somdy's poor lads," sed Sammy, "an a grand show they mak, an' fowk may weel be praad on 'em, but it gooas agean th' grain wi' me to think at sich hansom chaps, full o' life an' energy, should be banded together to kill or be killed, an' that's abaat what it comes to if its fairly reckoned up. Aw suppooas it's nescessary at it should be soa, but aw wish it wornt; an' it ud be a blessin if th' words ov th' old song could be acted on.

> "If I was King of France
>   Or what's better, Pope of Rome,
> I'd have no fighting men abroad,
>   No weeping maids at home.
> All the world should be at peace,
>   And if kings would show their might,
> I'd have those who make the quarrels be
>   The only men to fight."

Th' church an' castle wer visited, an' Philip pointed aght different interestin objects as they went along, an' th' new buildins to be seen ommost at ivvery turnin. Dewhirst's mill is a wonder in itsen. One wod fancy they could supply sewin cotton for all th' world an' have a stock left.

Then they trespassed on to private graands, but nubdy interfered, an' as they went on an' on, up rustic lanes,—across green meadows or sauntered bi th' watter side, it wor just one beauty after another, an' th' time went pleasantly by.

Sammy will long remember his visit to Skipton as one ov th' breetest, happiest times its been his priviledge to spend in his latter days.

---

"Nah, this is summat like a booat," sed Sammy, when Peter tuk him to luk at it.

H

"Aw've crossed th' Atlantic ooacean i' one at worn't as hansum as this," an' it wor a fine booat an' noa mistak. It wor th' biggest Sammy had ivver seen an' it wor painted to luk ommost as smart as a swingin booat at a Fair, an' ivverything abaat it wor as trim an' as cleean as a pin, except Crammer. Even Throstle had fixed hissen up a bit an' wor wearin a paper collar. Peter, too, wor shaved an' brushed up wol he lukt quite a different chap to what he wor when he left Leeds. Ther wor five or six other men on booard, an' they seemed to be ov a better class. Ther wor noa screw to th' tail end o' this booat like ther had been to th' Fly booats, but ther wor two old screws yoked to a rooap at th' forend.

"It's a pity," sed Sammy to Peter, when they wor fairly off, " at they dooant have better cattle to pool theas things."

"Ther's a varry mistakken nooation at fowk have getten abaat booat horses. They think at onny sooart ov an old frame is bowt for this wark, but it's net soa. They buy some o' th' best at they can ligg ther hands on, but th' wark is varry tryin an' they sooin begin to fall away. Drivers used to be a varry low, hardened, cruel lot, but ther's few o' them left an' they're pratty cloisly watched. When fowk say 'as silly as a booat horse,' they dooant know what they're tawkin abaat, for ther's few animals soa intelligent. They give 'em queer names sometimes—yond grey mare is called Cyclone, an' th' braan un is called Creeper, nawther name fits 'em varry weel, but they're a fine pair an' tha'll see they'll keep at that speed, barrin locks, until we get to Nelson, then we shall have to stop agean for a bit."

## CHAPTER ELEVENTH.

### NELSON AND BURNLEY.

TIME works wonders, an' onny body at wants to see one on 'em should goa to Nelson. We'd left Yorksher behund an' wor havin th' furst taste o' Lancasher. Peter sed Nelson had sprung up like a mushrum, but that's hardly a fair illustration; for altho' mushrums spring up varry sharply, they're allus varry tender an' barely aghtlast a day.

Twenty-five year sin, Nelson wor a collection ov a few ancient cottages, at lukt as if they'd getten lost an' hadn't enuff heart left in 'em to get onny farther. It wor Nelson near Colne at that day, but it's tother rooad abaat nah. Nelson's noa longer a ramblin village on a hill top, but a big, thrivin, bustlin taan. Ther's a covered market at wodn't disgrace onny Lancasher city, a theatre, far handsomer aghtside nor what Leeds or Bradford can booast. Mills at employ hundreds, an' rows ov substantial dwellings, a peep into onny on 'em enough to show at ther inside comforts are well cared for. Aw remember when a traveller, stranded at Nelson, wor in a pratty bad fix, unless he knew somdy.

But that's all altered nah. Cloise to th' station is th' Commercial Hotel, as perfect in its way as money an' knowledge can mak it. A chap at cannot be satisfied thear is hard to pleeas. An' th' fowk are net behind as regards knowin what's what. They've churches an' chapels, an' schooils sich as wod be a credit to onny place; an' a chap can find plenty to admire an' enjoy for a day or two, for although it has all th' advantages ov bein a taan, it hasn't lost all its country charm. Th' men an' wimmen arn't wizzened up as if they wor pinin for a breeath o' fresh air, an' th' lads an' lasses are as rooasy as if they'd nivver seen inside a factry, an' ther cheeks are soa plump wol they seem to spell 'puddin.'

Sammy an' his friends had a stroll raand an' as they wor passin a public haase at wor well up th' hill side, Peter stopt an' sed,

"Nah, Crammer, aw'll pay for a pint if tha dar goa in thear."

"Let's have howld o'th' brass an' aw'll let thi see whether aw dar goa in or net," sed Crammer.

"What's he been dooin?" sed Sammy. "He's been chawkin up an' hasn't paid his shot aw reckon."

"Nay, its war nor that. But aw see bi th' sign at th' same chap doesn't keep it nah, soa let's goa in an' tha shall hear th' tale," soa we all went in, an' when we wor sarved, Peter sed, "Nah, Throstle, tell Sammy that tale ha Crammer gat on th' spree at th' lanlord's expense."

"Aw can nobbut tell it as Crammer tell'd it to me, but if aw dooant tell it reight he can contradict me. It happened i' this way. Crammer wor here one time an' he wor aght ov a shop, an' bein a varry keen frost on, ther wor nowt for him to do i'th' booatin line, an' he called in here an axt th' lanlord if he'd strap him a pint, which ov coorse he'd moor sense,—but he sed he'd give him a job for a day or two, an' he could have his booard an' lodgins. Crammer jumpt at th' chonce for his inside wor soa empty wol his back booan grated agean th' buckle ov his belt. Th' lanlord went wi' him into th' cellar an' set him to shiftin some barrels abaat, an' ther wor two on 'em at wor abaat hawf full ov old ale, an' he thowt he'd empty one into tother to mak moor raam. He went upstairs to fotch a funnel, an' wol he wor away Crammer fell asleep aside o' th' gantry, wi' his heead lained agean th' barrel, an' his maath wide open. When th' lanlord coom back he missed Crammer but he started on to do th' job hissen, an' as it wor rayther dark he shoved th' funnel into Crammer's maath asteead o' into th' bung hoil, an' began drawin ale aght one barrel an', for owt he knew, teemin it into tother, an' he nivver fan aght his mistak until th' third bucketful, when Crammer began to run ovver, an' wakkened just i' time to prevent havin his throit bung'd up, an' when he gat onto his feet th' lanlord wor soa freetened at he ran up th' steps two at a time, but when Crammer proved to be noa war, he wanted to charge him for what he'd had, but at last he wor glad to give him a shillin to goa aght o' th' haase an' tell nubdy. He says he's nivver had as cheeap a doo sin then. But whether he's tell'd trewth or net, aw'll say nowt. He's thear to spaik for hissen."

"Well, Crammer," sed Sammy, "that tale an' another as bad owt to get thee three months at leeast."

"If aw wor thee, Sammywell, awd write some poetry abaat that."

"If tha thinks ther's onny poetry to be getten aght o' Crammer, tha mun try thisen an' tha'll find its as hard wark to write poetry as it is to keep aght o' debt when thi credits gooid. But aw think its time to shift us quarters. What's th' next move?"

"We're gooin on to Burnley throo here, but we shall goa bi rail for we want to get thear befoor th' booat, as we've some messages to 'liver, an' its ommost time we wor off," sed Peter.

"Yo can goa as yo've a mind, but when aw left hooam it wor for a yottin trip, an' it's baan to be awther yottin or trottin, an' aw'st travel noa other way, soa if yo like to leeav me yo can do soa."

Peter tried his best to perswade Sammy to goa wi' 'em, tellin him at he'd have plenty moor booatridin befoor he gat to th' far end, but he wor stupid, an' soa ther wor nowt for it but to leeav Sammy to goa on bi th' booat, an' they promised to meet him when he landed, an' if net, he'd be sewer to find 'em at th' Black Lion. An' soa they seperated.

Sammy sooin made friends wi' th' chaps on th' booat, an' altho he missed Peter a bit sometimes, yet, takkin it all together he enjoyed hissen better nor like. Ther wor constant changes i'th' scenery, an' lots o' places an' objects ov interest as they went along, tho he wor fain when Burnley wor come to, an' he lukt anxiously for them he expected to meet him, but he wor disappointed, for he saw nubdy but strangers, soa he set off at once to find th' Black Lion.

He hadn't expected to find Burnley sich a big place as it is, an' had noa idea at th' canal wor sich an important watter way. It ommost gooas raand hawf o' th' taan, an' ther's two rivers as weel, soa ther's noa want o' watter, but it's a pity it isn't purer. Rivers help trade varry mich but trade doesn't improve th' rivers.

Ther's churches an' chapels, an' markets an public Halls, an' signs o' prosperity ivverywhear, even th' pop shops luk respectable.

They dooant burn all th' smook they mak bi a long chawk, for sometimes its as mich as yo can do to see what time it is bi th' market clock, but whear ther's soa mich coil noa wonder ther's smook.

Sammy sooin made his way to th' Black Lion, but could see nowt ov his friends, soa he axt th' lanlord 'if three men had been thear, one on 'em born baght chin.'

"Hi, aw should think ther has, an' if tha's owt to do wi' 'em th' sooiner tha'rt off an' th' better. If tha wants to see 'em tha'll find 'em i' th' lock up."

"Whativver have they been dooin?"

"Th' poleece at had a warrant for 'em, says they're charged wi' killin a poor old chap at they'd enticed away throo his hooam at Bradforth. It seems they traced 'em as far as Keighley, but th' old chap's nivver been met wi' sin then, but somdy must ha fun his body for they sent his clooas to his widdy, an' shoo's set th' poleece on to ferret it aght. It'll be a hangin do for all three on 'em, ther's noa daat abaat it."

"Ha long is it sin they wor arrested?"

"Abaat an' haar sin. If yo'll tak my advice yo'll have nowt to do wi' it."

"Ther's been a mistak made, maister, an' aw'll give five shillin if yo'll send somdy wi' me to whear they are."

"Aw'll goa wi' yo misen," sed th' lanlord, an' off they went together.

Ill news travels fast. Ther wor a scoor o' fowk raand th' office door when Sammy gate thear, but th' poleece wodn't let onny goa in, but when he whispered a few words in his ear, Sammy an' th' lanlord wor passed throo.

"Thear they are," sed th' lanlord, pointin to Peter an' his two mates who wor sittin on a bench wi' ther heeads hung daan, an' guarded bi two officers. "Thear they are, like three lambs led to th' slowter," sed th' lanlord.

"They luk too sheepish to be lambs to my thinkin," sed Sammy, an' at th' saand ov his voice all three prisoners lawpt to ther feet, an' th' poleece seized 'em an' jowled ther heeads together, thinkin they wor tryin to mak an escape.

"Thear he is!" shaated Peter, "He's wick enuff! Come here, cussin, an' get us aght o' this hobble!"

"Silence!" sed th' bobbies.

Sammywell wor marched befoor a grey heeaded old gentleman at wor set up in a box, who lukt at him soa savage at he ommost began to believe he must ha been guilty o' summat. Then he wor axt his name, an' when he left hooam, an' ha it coom to pass at his clooas had been sent to his wife, minus his carcase? An' Sammywell tell'd just what had happened, an' ivverything wor soa plain an' straight forrad at th' magistrate sed it wor evidently a false alarm, an' it gave him mich pleasure to discharge the prisoners, an' he complimented th' poleece for ther assiduity an' wor only sorry at ther trouble had been wasted, an' then he gave Sammy a lectur, an' tell'd him at he owt to be thankful at his three comrades hadn't put him aght o' th' way, an' he hoped it ud be a warnin to him as long as he lived, net to goa abaat disguised as a gentleman onny moor; an' then he directed one o' th' poleece to goa an' braik th' news as gently as possible to Mistress Grimes, at her husband wor still alive an' hearty, an' unfortunately, that wor all they could do in the matter.

When they gate aghtside, one o'th' poleece,—th' same at had arrested 'em,—went back wi' 'em to th' Black Lion, an' they all indulged in some refreshment ov which they wor soorly i' need.

"Mistress Grimes gave me a letter befoor aw set off," sed th' poleeceman. "It's for Mister Captain Peter Garlick, Canal Booat," an' he handed it to him.

"That letter's intended for me!" sed Sammywell, "my wife's noa business to be sendin letters to her cussin wol awm alive!"

"But tha mun understand tha worn't alive when this wor written. Aw'll see what it says at onnyrate," an' Peter oppened it an' read,

*Deer cussin Captain Peter—*

*I write theas few lines to thank yo for sendin Sammywell's clooas, they'll cut up nicely for Jerrymiar. Dooant bother to send him here for we've just cleeaned daan an' he'll do as weel whear he is for he could nivver rest comfortable at hooam. Send his spyglass an' owt else he's left at's worth owt. Aw expect he'll miss me nah. Awr haase is varry quiet withaat him, an' aw allus like quietness, but all's for th' best when it ends weel. Aw hooap tha'll ax him if he knows owt abaat them five sovrins 'at wor hid i' th' metal teahpot for they arn't thear nah, an' at his peril he shows his face i' this fowld withaat 'em. Hepsabah has getten some new clooas an' black suits her. Tell deer Sammywell to send his stificat for we can't get th' club brass till he does. Aw've sent a poleece after him but aw shouldn't like him takkin up. Mistress Sparks 'at lives at Tumlin Hill browt me some scarrin stooan yesterdy an' shoo axt me to send her kind love to Sammywell, but shoo's a hippycrit soa aw havn't sent it for* ther's one at her own haase can do wi' all th' love shoo's getten so noa moor at present.

*Mally Grimes thi own cussin an' Sammywell's widdy.*

*Hepsabah says shoo nivver saw onnybody tak rubble wi' moor pleasur but shoo doesn't know ha aw freeat when awm asleep. Awm just gooin to start bakin curran cake an' aw've getten a bottle o' rum. dooant tell S——. tha knows who aw mean.*

"Nah, tha knows all at's in it, an' aw dooant know what tha thinks abaat it, Sammywell, but aw think tha owt to be shamed o' thisen to treeat a woman like Mally i' th' way tha does. Dooant yo think soa, Mister poleeceman?" sed Peter.

"Aw think it's scandlas," he sed, "If awd my way awd fine him glasses raand."

"Hear, hear!" sed Crammer.

"If awd known what aw know nah," sed Sammy, "awd ha stopt i' Nelson for a wick, an' yo should all ha been lockt up on suspicion. An' when aw get back hooam aw'll let somdy know what aw think abaat ther conduct. Aw'll pay 'em back i' ther own coin——"

"Tha's nivver paid me that five shillin tha promised me for showin thi whear to find thi mates," sed th' lanlord.

"Noa, aw hav'nt,—but aw will do,—an' aw'll mak it fifteen if tha'll get 'em all takken back agean.'

"Nay, nay! That wod be too bad. Aw think things have turned aght varry weel, an' if tha'll be five shillin to my five we'll have a reight dooment," sed th' lanlord.

"That's varry fair," sed Peter, " an' tha knows, Sammy, it'll raillee be mi cussin Mally 'at's treatin, becoss tha knows tha gat that brass aght o'th' teah pot."

"Thee mind thi own business, Captain Peter Garlick! Tha'd better keep thy nooas aght o' awr Mally's teah pot. Aw've had bother enuff wi' thi, an' if it worn't for th' relationship between us aw wod'nt goa wi' thi another yard!"

"Tha can suit thisen, Sammywell."

"Nay, aw cannot, or else awd punce yo all aght o'th' hoil! But here, lanlord, tak this ten shillin, an' let's have a knife an' fork drinkin, an' yo can affooard to bring us a drop o' summat to be gooin on wi' aght o' that."

Th' lanlord put th' brass in his pocket an' hurried off to give th' order, an' Throstle struck up "For he's a jolly good fellow!" an' they all joined in.

They'd a merry time wol it lasted, but th' booat wor to start for Wigan at six o'clock, soa after helpin th' lanlord to put th' poleeceman to bed they bid gooid-bye an' wended ther way to th' dock whear they faand th' booat all ready an' in a few minnits they wor continin ther trip.

## CHAPTER TWELFTH.

#### WANDERING ON TO WIGAN.

IF yo've ivver been to Burnley, yo've heeard ov Gaunow. When Sammywell wor at Skipton he'd heeard fowk tawk abaat Foulbridge tunnel, but owing to circumstances 'at its better to say nowt abaat, he passed through it unbeknownst, but he made up his mind 'at he'd see Gaunow tunnel, or if he couldn't see it, he'd have his wits abaat him when he went through.

It wornt long befoar th' horse wor takken off th' booat, an' what wor his surprise to find a steeam tug waitin' to tak em through. Gooin' throo a canal tunnel isn't a thing to be recommended to fowk 'at's seekin' fresh air, but onnybody 'at's fanciful to owt 'at's flaysum couldn't do better. It wor nobbut hawf a mile long, but that's quite long enuff, an' bi th' time Sammy saw dayleet agean he forgave Peter for net wakkenin' him up at Foulbridge. When they'd getten through Peter sed, "Wes't be at Church directly," an' sewer enuff they wor, but it wornt th' sooart ov a church Sammy expected. Church is a fine taan, an' one o'th' receivin' stations for th' canal compny. Ther wor a short stop wol they put some stuff off an' tuk some moor on, but Peter sed it wor their best plan to stop whear they wor, which they did, an' as darkness wor gently shuttin' aght all surrandins they sattled daan to mak th' best o' things wol they gat to Blackburn. Yo'd hardly expect to find Nova Scotia at Blackburn, but it is.

Hillock locks wor passed an' then they turned in. Sammywell had a comfortable shake daan an' wor sooin asleep, but he didn't rest varry weel for he kept dreeamin' 'at Mally wor commin' on a heearse to fotch him; an' when they gat to Whittle Springs, they all gat off, for although they'd had nowt to do but rest, yet ther's relief in a change, an' beside they felt like refreshin th' inner man agean.

It's a grand spot is Whittle Springs, an' ther's some pleasur gardens thear, wi' bowlin' green, an' lots ov amusements. It wor rayther sooin for visitors, but they managed to get a tidy braikfast, an' then Sammy an' Throstle laiked Peter an' Crammer at bowls for who paid next. Considerin' 'at ther wornt one i'th' lot 'at had play'd bowls befoor, they managed to get a goood deeal o' fun aght on it, but when Sammy felt sewer 'at his side wor winnin', one ov his balls wor missin' They sowt all raand for it, but they couldn't find it, an' then Sammy declared Crammer had swallered it, but altho' Crammer oppened his maath to let 'em see 'at he wor innocent, Sammy stuck to it, an' soa they went back to th' canal wharf, an' as ther wor a Fly booat just startin' for Wigan they stept abooard.

"It's a lazy sooart ov a life is this," sed Sammy, "but idleness they say is nowt worth unless it's weel follered, soa he pickt aght a cosy corner an' lit his pipe, an' gave way to meditation. An' ther wor plenty for him to meditate abaat. He remembered Critchly Prince, that sturdy Lancashire poet;—an' Charles Swain, that sweet singer;—an' Ernest Jones, who made Lancashire ring wi' his politics, but will live i' futur ages in his poetry. An' then he fell to communin' wi' Edwin Waugh, an' Sam Laycock —all past into that unknown whear we are hastenin' Ben Brierley—old veteran,—still cheers us, nah an' then, wi' some ov his wise an' witty sketches. Ther shooin are ommost all empty, an' ther doesn't seem to be onny feet ready to fill 'em. Ther may be some risin up 'at will prove as goood,—nay, even better, but they'll have to climb long an' hard befoor they can mak their mark aboon them 'at's deeply cut i'th' rock ov a people's love.

Sammywell wor left alooan in his glory, for Peter an' his mates seemed to be tired aght, an' little happened 'at's worth tellin' until they coom to Wigan, an' then Sammywell raased hissen, an' Peter coom to point aght an' explain what wor interestin'. Stacks o' coil wor thear 'at must have been into th' thaasands ov tons;—an' th' locks fairly bewildered him.

"Tha did reight to tell me to bring mi kays to oppen th' locks wi'," sed Sammywell, "but aw'd noa idea o' seein' owt like this. Twenty three locks, one after another, for aw've caanted 'em! It's stupendous!" an' when Peter pointed aght th' Bridges an' explained ha' they'd sattled owing to th' mines under 'em, an' even th' canal itsen had sunk, an' showed ha' all had been rebuilt an' reconstructed, an' th' canal dredged until th' biggest booats could sail, even when looadened daan to th' watter's edge, he could say nowt but "Wonderful!" He wor fairly lost i' admiration, when Throstle struck up,

> "Down in a coal mine underneath the ground,
> Where a ray of sunlight never can be found;
> Digging dusky diamonds all the season round,
> Down in a coal mine, underneath the ground."

It didn't need onnybody to tell 'em 'at they wor

in a big taan when they gate to Wigan. Ivvery whear wor signs ov wealth,—corn mills,—cotton factrys,—faandry, an' machine shops on all sides; Railway stations, — a fine river spanned wi' bridges. A parish church 'at's worth a journey to see, an' other churches here an' thear,—a taan hall, cloth hall, sessions hall, corn exchange, banks, barracks, an' gaol;—schooils ov all sooarts an' coil dust an' smook enuff on th' faces yo meet to mak yo feel ashamed 'at yo' arn't workin' too.

"Here we are an' here aw meean to stop wol to-morn," sed Sammywell. Th' rest on 'em wor quite willin, and soa Throstle an' Crammer wor sent off to spend ther time as they thowt fit, an' Peter an' Sammy went throo one place to another seein' all 'at wor to be seen. After makkin' arrangements for a neet's lodgins an' weel fortified wi' a beefsteak an' fried oonions, they went to seek some entertainment to pass th' evenin', an' sooin they landed in a concert hall,—a varry respectable, weel conducted place, as far as one could judge. Ther wor a varry mixed performance, an' if nowt wor new, nowt wor commonplace nor objectionable.

"Let's goa," sed Sammy, when it had getten ten o'clock, "aw should like to be off i' gooid time i'th' mornin."

They hadn't goan varry far when they saw a craad o' fowk follerin' some poleece who wor

huggin summat 'at all seemed interested in.—
They pushed ther way through, an' on a hand
ambulance they saw a seet 'at filled 'em wi'
horror. A lifeless body ov a young woman
drippin' wi' weet, her eyes starin', an' her lips
smilin' as if shoo'd welcomed her release. "Just
been taken from the river," sed a man who
seemed to be in charge. "It's a thaasand pities,"
sed another, "for shoo used to be a nice respectable lass, but shoo went to th' bad, an' this is th'
end on her."

"It's to be hooaped 'at th' chap at gate her
into trouble willn't get off scot free," sed a
woman at stood by, "he led her off when shoo
wor little moor nor a child, an' when he'd done
wi' her he cast her off. Aw shouldn't like to be
he his shoon this neet! God forgive her!"

"Amen," sed Sammywell, an' together Peter
an' him turned away, as he repeated theas lines
'at seemed to have been written on her.

"Guilty no doubt, and died in her dishonour!
    She knew no friends save men these many years,
Her best and worst. I only look upon her—
    They kissed with smiles, but have for her no tears.
Did the last spark of life that lit these ashes
    Drown in the wine she drank unto the lees?
Or did dark eyes look out 'neath painted lashes
    To childhood's home among the waving trees?

Ere o'er her being came the last death quiver,
Perhaps she heard across the shining river,
  "God's holy love was made for such as these."

Shameless she was, indeed, and steeped in sinning;
  Cold virtue, scorning, passed her quickly by
Upon the arm of him whose voice so winning
  Had caused her fall.  In vain for her to cry
For pity or for mercy,—close the curtain,
  She must not look upon her home firelight;
But one false step—the end for her is certain—
  Shut her forever out into the night.
Among her rags, as she lies calmly sleeping,
A token I will place within her keeping—
  One fragrant rosebud, pure and snowy white."

They shook hands, when they coom to whear they wor to spend th' neet, an' seperated saddened, an' sorrowful.

## CHAPTER THIRTEENTH.

##### NEARING THE END.

NAWTHER Sammywell nor Peter wor able to shake off entirely th' sad feelin at wor caused bi th' memory ov what they'd seen th' neet befoor. After braikfast they tuk ther way daan to th' canal, whear, as they expected, Throstle an' Crammer wor waitin. Ther wor noa booat just ready to start, soa they spent ther time rambling abaat an' watchin th' chaps at wor looadin an unlooadin th' barges. Fowk at judge canals bi what can be seen at Leeds or Bradford have but a poor idea ov what they railly are. If it worn't for th' abscence ov sails a stranger might easily mistak Wigan for a sea-pooart.

Booath Sammywell an' Peter lukt varry respectable, especially Sammy, an' Throstle an' Crammer seemed to have been takkin extra pains wi' ther get up, an' Sammy wor anxious to know th' reason why.

"Th' next stoppin place for us is Burscough, an' that's th' reason," sed Peter. "Tha sees they get paid thear, an' they've booath summat commin to 'em, an' they like to luk as weel as they can when they goa to th' office. They'll leeav us when we get thear, for that's whear they live when they're at hooam, soa tha'll have to luk aght for thi spy glass if tha wants it, but it railly isn't worth botherin abaat. Tha'd better let Crammer have it for th' children to laik wi."

"A'a! tha doesn't know thi cussin Mally if tha thinks aw dar face her withaat it. Shoo'd nivver spaik to me agean withaat beginnin 'If tha hadn't lost thi spy glass,' or 'If we nobbut had that talescope;' aw should nivver hear th' last on it."

"Well, tha should know th' best,—but here's a booat ready to start."

They wor sooin on ther journey agean, an' all sat daan together at one end o'th' booat. They wor varry quiet for they knew at th' time wor near for a seperation, an' they'd getten a likin for one another, when Throstle burst aght into song—

> In this world of care and sorrow,
>   There are moments of delight,
> Though to-day is dull, to-morrow
>   May be sunny, warm and bright.
> Be contented in your station,
>   Blaming fortune will not mend,

Make a firm determination
  To fight bravely to the end.

    Let your motto be 'endeavour,'
      Persevering in the fray;
    Hoping on, despairing never,
      You shall surely win the day.

Friends you loved may go and leave you,
  When you most their presence crave;
Some you trusted may deceive you,—
  Then it is you must be brave.
Do not let your courage falter,
  Let your aim be truth and right,
Soon the clouds of gloom will alter,
  To a heaven all blue and bright.

    Let your motto be 'endeavour,'
      Persevering in the fray;
    Hoping on,—despairing never,
      You shall surely win the day.

"If awd a pint at th' front o' me nah, Throstle, awd ax thi to sup," sed Sammy, "but tha mun tak th' will for th' deed this time, but if ivver aw meet thi at Bradford, tha shall have th' best o' owt tha likes. Nah, Crammer, has ta nowt to say?"

But he shook his heead. "Awm net like Throstle, aw nivver could do owt i'th' poetry line. Aw once tried but aw nobbut gate four lines."

"Well let's have 'em!" An Crammer puttin on a varry solemn phiz resited

> Aw'm a poor workin' man
> An' mi name it is Crammer;
> Aw am as aw am,
> An' aw cant be noa ammer.

"Is that all on it?" sed Sammy.

"Eeah, that's all, aw did try another verse, but aw couldn't mak onny sense on it."

"Dooant try onny moor, if tha does tha'll spoil it. If tha leeaves it as it is fowk 'll gie thi credit for knowin' when to stop, whether they forgie thi for startin' or net. It's thy turn, Peter."

"Nay, yo' mun let me pass. Aw nivver could sing i' mi life, an' aw nivver knew but one piece o' poetry, an' that wor 'Mary had a little lamb,' an' aw daat whether aw know that reight."

"Get agate, we'll excuse thi if tha braiks daan," soa Peter put his studdyin' cap on an' then began.

> "Mary had a little lamb,
> Its fleece wor white entirely,
> An' ivverywhear that Mary went,
> That sheep went too."

"That's th' warst 'at aw ivver heeard!" sed Sammy. It's a blessin' that's all tha knows, an' be sewer tha keeps it to thisen for th' futer, an' nivver try to leearn onny moor," an' he gate up an' wor leeavin 'em i' disgust, when he happened to catch th' seet ov a bottle neck stickin aght ov Peter's pocket, soa he thowt better on it, an' set daan agean.

Peter twigg'd what Sammy wor after, but he kept him waitin' for ivver soa long, but at last he handed it raand an' they all drank one another's health as long as it lasted.

Sammy set ponderin' for a bit, an' then he sed, "Peter, aw think aw owt to write Mally a letter, —shoo'll be expectin' one aw know, altho' shoo did send yond poleece after me. If it had been a man 'at had sent him on sich a eearand as that they'd ha' made him pay for't, an' deearly too, but it seems to me 'at they'll let wimmen do owt. Aw have some paper an' a leead pencil an' that'll do nicely, an' aw can pooast it at Burscough, soa he went into a quiet corner an' wrate.

*On the deep Blue C.(anal,)*

*Mistress Mally Grimes, wife ov Sammywell Grimes, who is still alive an' kickin' as this leeaves me at present.*

*Dear Mally,*

*Cussin Peter received thy letter an' wishes me to say 'at he doesn't thank thi for it. Aw hooap tha'll tell Hepsabah 'at if aw catch her wearin' black* looas i' awr haase aw'll goa straight aght an' buy Ferrymier a drum an' a whistle an' a pair o' clappers an' a stick o' spenishjuice for Sunday. Tha can bake as mich curran cake as tha likes, an' dooant oppen that bottle o' rum wol aw come, th' doctors say at ther's a deeal o' mycrobes i' rum, an' if tha has noa thowt for thisen aw have. If them five sovrins wor takken aght o' that metal teapot after aw left hooam aw dooant see ha tha can suspicion me. Varry likely they've getten changed, an' if soa tha'll have hard wark to find 'em. Dooant think onny moor abaat 'em for moneys the rooit ov all evil. Aw've missed thee varry mich an' had a nice quiet time, for which aw'm thankful. Peter says he'll be sooary to part wi' me an' sympathises wi' me varry mich. Tell Mistress Sparks 'at aw'm thankful for her kind love an' scaarin' stooan. Yottin' is a grand institution for idlin' yor time away. Hoopin' to find thi at hooam, an' yet have to seek thi at awr Hepsabah's,

*Believe me thy original lawful wedded husband,*

*Sammywell Grimes, C. D. (Commodoor.)*

Ther wor nowt ov mich importance tuk place befoor they coom i' seet o' Burscough, except ha' fidgetty an' anxious Crammer an' Throstle seemed to get as they drew nearer. They wor booath ready to jump off as sooin as th' booat coom near, an' Sammy wor capt to see a hansum woman wi' two fine childer come hurryin' up to Crammer an' fling her arms raand th' middle section ov his throttle, an' kiss him agean an' agean. "Well, that licks dol!" he sed to Peter. "Do theas booatmen have wives an' childer like other fowk?"

"They've ommost all wives, but th' wimmen have th' childer, mooastly."

"Why, shoo seems as praad on him as if he wor an Adonis."

"Well, tha sees he's her Donis, an' that's ivverything to her. He's a varry hardworkin' chap, an' soa is Throstle, sithee! his wife has come to meet him too, an' he's getten one child on his back an' one bi awther hand. Mun, ther's as true love to be fun in a booatman's cottage as i'th' grandest mansion i'th' land."

"Aw believe soa. Nay, awm sewer soa! It's love 'at brings happiness, ther's noa daat abaat it. Love they say is blind, but aw nivver thowt it wor, but aw must admit aw think it's rayther shortseeted when it comes to sich as Crammer. It calls to my mind what a young woman says,

"If love is true I need not care,
  That fortune's gifts are very few:
Love has perception rich and rare,
  If love be true.

Yet once I wished my eyes were blue,
  That I had waves of auburn hair,—
My face a tint of beauty's hue.

Since love has come my life to share,
    From faith and hope, all fear withdrew;
Love will not see I am not fair,
    If love be true.

Burscough is a wonderful place. This is whear th' canal horses are kept, on a big farm belangin' th' compny, an' all ther provender is stored here.

A chap wor hard at work mixin' bran an' corn an' beans, an' chop, enuff it seemed to fodder a army. When Sammy expressed his surprise at findin' sich a lot o' fine cattle, he laft. "Why, sur," he sed, "wod yo' believe 'at this compny pays forty, an' as mich as sixty guineas apiece for theas horses?"

"Well," sed Sammy, "if awd been tell'd soa befoor awd seen what aw have, aw should ha' had mi daats abaat it, but awm foorced to believe it nah. But ha' is it 'at aw nivver see onny on th' canal banks 'at luk like theas?"

"Aw cant tell you that, maister," he sed, "for th' horses yo see here were some on 'em on th' bank to-day an' some will goa on agean directly. Happen yo've nivver takken mich nooatice, an' yo know, fine feathers mak fine burds an' a fine harness sets off a poor horse, an' fine harness is what we've noa use for."

"But dooant booatmen treeat 'em badly sometimes?"

"Ther's gooid an' bad amang booatmen as amang all sooarts, but if onny one is known to ill use a horse he gets his ticket o' leeav, an' that sattles him."

"Whear's my spy glass?" axt Sammy, as he suddenly recollected at he hadn't seen it.

"Crammer must have it," sed Peter, "let's goa an' see."

They started off an' wor sooin at th' cottage whear Crammer lived, an' a nice, cleean, comfortable hooam it wor. Crammer wor set at th' table wi' one child on his knee an' another at his elbow, an' i' th' front on him wor a pie,—an' it *wor* a pie! It must ha been made in a weshin bowl;—each o' th' childer had a piece o' th' crust as big as a clog soil, in its fist, an' Crammer wor divin into th' dish, an' bringin aght whooal puttates an' chunks o' mait ommost th' size ov a child's heead, an' they vanished as if bi magic. When Sammy wor informed at his spy glass wor on th' booat, they bid gooid day, an' left him to struggle wi' his meal.

"We shall have to luk sharp if we meean to catch that booat," sed Peter, soa they struck a bee line for it, an' just ovvertuk it as it wor leeavin. Sammy made sewer at his talescope wor safe, an' then suggested at summat to ait wod'nt be amiss, an' Peter led th' way into th' cabin, whear they had as mich stew an' cake as they wanted.

"This is th' end o' th' journey as far as th' canal is consarned," sed Peter, "we shall'nt stop agean till we get to Bank Hall an' that's Bootle, an Bootle's Liverpool we may say, an' th' tramcar will tak thi to onny pairt o' Liverpool tha wants to goa to. But we shall have another neet on th' booat."

"A neet or two moor or less maks noa matter to me," sed Sammy, "for nah at awm used to it, aw can live as comfortably on th' booat as on dry land."

They gat some secks an' made a comfortable corner whear they could loll an' rest an' be aght ov ivverybody's way, an' leetin ther pipes they puffed away to ther heart's content, but bein rayther tired, an' undisturbed, an' th' day bein varry sultry, they dooazed off, an' when they wakkened th' mooin wor shinin an' all wor calm an' peeaceful.

A mug o' hot coffee an' some cold beef an breead wor noa bad supper, an' after another smook they went below an' prepared to sleep wol mornin.

When they wakkened, another seet surprised Sammy. Booats ivverywhear,—big warehaases, stooary aboon stooary wol it made his neck ache to luk up at 'em. Ivvery whear wor bustle. It wor early, but they decided to land, an' havin bowt a mornin paper off a little newslad, Sammy lapt up his spy glass, an' tuckin it under his arm, they went ashore, an' went to get a braikfast, which wod be th' last meal they'd have together for a long time. Peter had to mak enquiries abaat th' carpet bag, but he arranged to meet Sammy i' th' afternooin at th' General Managers office, Pall Mall; an they seperated, Sammy delighted wi' th' trip an' anxious to get back hooam, an' Peter, pleeased to see ha mich he'd enjoyed it, they parted, for th' time bein, on th' mooast friendly terms, an' if a feelin ov bitterness had ivver had a place in his breast on Mally's accaant, it gave place to a feelin ov thankfulness at he'd two cussins asteead o' one.

## CHAPTER FOURTEENTH.

##### CONCLUSION.

AGHTSIDE London, ther's noa English city 'at has as monny an' as varied seets as Liverpool. Sammy sooin fan his way daan to th' landin' stage an' wor lucky enuff to be just i' time to see th' steeamship Kensington arrive from America. It's a wonderful improvement 'at's been made 'at enables big passenger vessels to come an' discharge ther passengers an' luggage direct into th' city asteead o' havin' to stop 'ith river an' send 'em all off bi tenders. Ther wor nearly a thaasand fowk landed, but although Sammy watched wol th' last wor ashore, he didn't see one he knew, soa after a bit he thowt he'd just have a trip to New Brighton. It wor varry different to ridin' on a canal booat an' th' change made it moor appreciated.

He'd just getten set daan i' th' saloon when he nooaticed a middle aged woman wi' a child

J

in her arms an' three little childer draggin at her gaon, an' shoo seemed to be lukkin aght for somdy.

Shoo noa sooiner saw Sammy nor shoo rushed up to him an' sed, "A'a! Noah, aw've fun thi at last!" an' shoo threw one arm raand his neck an' burried her face in his shirt-front.

"Yo're mistakken, Mistress!" he sed, as sooin as he could get his wind, "Awm noa Noah,— net aw marry! My name's Sammywell!"

"A'a, aw wonder ha tha can fashion to say sich a thing after sendin for me to come here to meet thi, an' thi own child i' mi arms, at tha's nivver set thi e'en on until nah, for he worn't born when tha went away an' left us! Come, kuss yor daddy, doys!" shoo sed to th' childer, an' all three climb'd ovver him an' kussed him i' spite o' all he could do.

"If yo dooant tak theas young imps off me, Mistress, aw'll pitch 'em into th' watter. Goa abaat yor business an' let me alooan. Aw know nooan on yo, an' what's mooar, aw dooant want to!"

Bi this time ther wor quite a craad gethered raand 'em.

"What's to do, Mistress?" axt one o' th' wimmen passengers.

"Mi heart's fairly brokken," sed th' woman, "We've com'd all th' way throo America, to meet mi husband, an' nah he'll nawther own me nor his childer, an' onnybody can see who they tak after!" an' shoo brast aght cryin.

"Shame on him!" they cried, "Awd mak him own 'em an' keep 'em too if aw had him to deeal wi'," sed one, an' things began to luk serious.

"Aw tell yo ther's some tarrible mistak," sed Sammy, "Aw nivver saw this woman nor her childer befoor i' mi life! They're nowt akin to me!"

"A'a, he's a hardened wretch!" sed another woman, shakkin her umberel in his face, "As if a woman could'nt own her own husband an' th' father ov her childer! If aw wor his wife awd give him i' charge as sooin as ivver aw gate on tother side!"

Sammy wor fast amang it, for he could nawther tell ha he'd getten into sich a hobble nor ha to get aght on it. It wor a varry queer fix to be in. Thear he wor stood wi' th' woman dandlin th' child i'th' front on him an' tother three hung fast to his coit tails, an' all th' passengers craaded raand when th' booat stopt, an' ther wor a rush to land, but they all seem'd bent on seein th' upshot on it, an' when he landed, wi' th' woman an' childer still clingin to him it lukt as if he'd be likely to be roughly handled amang 'em, but just then a chap coom forrad an' sed,

"Heigh up, Rachel! Here aw am, lass!

Aw've been waitin aboon an haar!" an' withaat moor to do he gave her a kuss an' tuk th' child in his arms.

"A'a, Noah!" sed th' woman, as shoo brast aght laffin, "aw've been takkin another chap for thee! Sithee, this is him!" shoo sed, pointin to Sammy.

"Tha must be gooin blind aw think," sed Noah, "why, that chaps old enuff to be mi father!"

"Well, tha needn't luk mad, for ther's nowt noa war as it happens, an' tha knows its three months sin aw saw thi an' tha mud ha aged a deeal i' that time. Yo'll excuse me, weant yo, maister?" shoo sed to Sammy.

"Aw'll excuse all th' family on yo if yo'll nobbut let me goa abaat mi business," an' he elbowed his way throo th' craad as weel as he could.

"Aw'st be foorsed to admit at awr Mally's reight when shoo says 'at aw ammot fit to be trusted bi misen. If yond chap hadn't turned up when he did, aw'st ha been in a bonny pickle. Still aw connot help sympathisin wi' Noah, for it connot be pleasant to have a wife at's sich a poor memory!"

Ther's plenty o' sands at New Brighton, an' if ther's mich ov a breeze yor likely to be made aware on it. Th' old fort stands whear it did, but whether it wor intended for use or ornament aw dooant know, but it seems to be nawther. Fine big places ov amusement have been provided, an' ther's a row ov 'Tea an' shrimps,—ninepence' shops 'at wodn't be mich ov a loss if they'd to be carried aght to seah an' sunk, or buried under th' sand. Ivvery shop has its piano an' its private corners, whear yo can be waited on bi tawdry dressed young wimmen 'at luk as if a gooid wesh an' a neet's rest wod be a treat they hadn't had latly.

Ther wor some immitation niggers workin hard to addle as mich as ud pay for ther clooas weshin', but judgin' bi th' way they seemed to be rewarded when aw wor thear, awm feeard they'll be worn aght befoor weshed.

An' enterprisin' Yorksherman has put up a Switchback an' seems to be dooin' varry weel wi' it. Sammywell had a ride on it, an' it reminded him ov his own life's journey,—plenty o' ups an' daans, an' at th' finish, just whear he'd started an' summat aght o' pocket.

He didn't stop long, an' wor sooin back at Liverpool. Then he went throo St. George's Hall, an' had a luk throo th' Art Gallery an' th' Public Library, an' wandered up an' daan th' streets a bit, an' then went into a Temperance Hotel to get a snack, an' bi that time it wod be time to meet Peter. (Sammywell allus maks a practice to tail off his vacation at a Temperance

Hotel;—net 'at they suit him as weel as some other sooarts, but he fancies it ensures him ov a better chonce ov a welcome when he lands hooam.)

"What have yo' i'th' aitin' line, mistress?" he axt.

"Why," shoo sed, studyin' it ovver, "let me see. Yo' can have ham, or yo' can have eggs,—or yo' can have ham an' eggs."

"That's varry nice, mistress, but aw've had soa mich ham an' bacon latly wol if aw get onny moor awst nivver be able to luk a pig i'th' face agean."

"Well, th' pigs 'll nooan freeat abaat that," shoo sed, "but if yo' connot mak a meal o' ham an' eggs an' gooid breead an' butter, yo'll be like to try another shop."

"Let's have some coffee an' a buttered cake then," he sed, an' he managed to satisfy hissen for fourpence, which wor varry reasonable.

When he gate to th' office ov th' canal compny, he faand Peter waitin', an' after a bit he wor introduced to th' manager, a varry nice gentleman, an' he thanked him for his kindness an' tell'd him he'd enjoyed his trip furstrate; an' th' manager sed 'he wor glad on it, an' he hoped th' canal wodn't be onny worse for it,' an' they shook hands an' parted th' best o' friends.

"Ha's ta gooan on?" axt Sammy when Peter an' him wor aghtside.

"Oh, furstrate. Th' carpet bag wor at Bootle, an' it seems th' directions had been lost off it, an' we oppened it to see what wor in, an' mak sewer ther wor nowt brokken, but ther wor nowt to braik except a child's feedin' bottle, for ther wor nowt else in but some dried mint an' pennyroyal, an' a quarter ov a pund o' Jarmen yeast 'at had gooan bad."

"Why, whativver made her put Jarmen yeast in?"

"Nay, aw dooant know, unless shoo happen thowt 'at if it fell into th' watter it mud help it to rise agean."

"An' what does Abagail Cornstock say? Aw suppooas yo' let her know when yo' faand it?"

"Eeah, we sent a lad wi' it at once, but when he coom back, he sed 'at as sooin as shoo saw what wor in it, shoo tell'd him to tak it back, for shoo'd ha nooan on it, an' becoss he wodn't, shoo threw it after him into th' street an' it's thear yet for owt we know."

"Soa its takken three men a wick to hunt up an old carpet bag 'at wornt worth havin'?"

"That's soa;—it wor worth nowt when it wor faand, but ther's noa tellin' ha mich it ud ha been worth if it had been lost. But this compny has a reputation to keep up, an' ther's nivver owt lost. But aw expect tha'll be wantin' to get hooam agean;—has ta getten thi spyglass?"

"Eeah, that's all reight. Tha'll see me off aw reckon?"

"Nowt'll suit me better. Come on."

They'd varry few minnits to wait for a train, soa after gooin' in th' refreshment raam, to compare th' clock wi' Peter's watch, they shook hands an' parted; Peter promisin' to send Sammy's box to Bradford as sooin as he gate back to Leeds.

It wor nobbut hawf past five when th' train started an' at eight o'clock Sammy landed safe an' saand at Bradford.

---

When Sammy stept on th' platform he wor surprised to find Mally an' Hepsabah an' little Jerrymier all waitin' to receive him. He couldn't tell ha they'd getten to know what train he'd come on, until Mally tell'd him 'at Peter had sent a telegram.

Mally couldn't help showin' ha pleeased shoo wor to see him safe back agean, especially as he lukt soa smart an' respectable, an' Hepsabah wor donned in a new blue gaon wi' a bunch o' May blossom under her chin, an' a hat on, as big as a small teah table, all bedizenned wi' feathers an' flaars; an' as they walked aght o'th' station,— Jerrymier gooin' furst wi' th' talescope, an' Sammy follerin, wi' Mally howd o' one arm an

Hepsabah clingin' to tother,—th' pooarters touch ther cap nebs as they passed an' th' Station maister claated a lad at side o'th' heead becoss he didn't get aght o'th' gate.

All th' wimmen i'th' fowld coom aght to see 'em as they went in hooam, an' they all agreed 'at they couldn't tell whativver Mally could be thinkin' on to let her husband goa rammelin' abaat, bi a wick at a time, an' then tak him back hooam agean, as if nowt wor.

But Mally knew th' sooart ov a chap shoo had to deeal wi an they did'nt, an that made all th' difference, an aw allus think at them wives ats fond o' suspectin other wimmen's husbands cannot have varry mich confidence i ther own. Ther can be noa perfect love withaat perfect trust, an aw nivver met a jaylus husband or wife, at had'nt summat i' ther own heart at they wor careful to keep aght oth' seet. But jaylussy is one o' them things at even philosphers differ abaat, for one tells us "Love is genuine as long as it is jealous," an another says "Jealousy is impossible with perfect love," soa thear yo have it an yo mun sooart it for yorsen.

Th' drinkin' wor ready an' they wor ready for it, but Jerrymier wodn't be content until he'd seen th' talescope, soa Sammy unlapt it, an' then explained 'at as it had been noa use as a spy glass, he'd getten it altered into a squirter to swill th' winders, but Mally declared shoo'd nivver put it to noa sich use for it ud do varry weel for a rollin' pin, but Hepsabah sed it ud be a shame to spoil it, an' if he'd give it her, shoo'd have it made into a stand for a parrafin lamp. Soa it wor agreed 'at Hepsabah should have it.

After th' drinkin' Sammy had to relate as mich ov his gooins on as he thowt it wor advisable for 'em to know, an' then he tuk Mally to tawk to, abaat sendin' th' poleece after him, an' writin' sich a letter to Peter.

Then Hepsabah explained 'what a shock it had been to her mother when th' bundle o' clooas coom, an' th' naybors wor all sewer 'at he wor draanded or summat, an' they made sich a ta do abaat it wol th' poleece gate to hear on it, an' for want o' summat better to do they'd made summat aght o' nowt.'

"But what abaat that letter to Peter?" axt Sammy.

"Thee say nowt abaat that letter, an' aw'll say nowt abaat that metal teahpot," sed Mally, soa Sammy wor fain to have it soa, an' when Hepsabah an' Jerrymier wor biddin' 'em gooid neet, he gave his gronson a thripny bit, an' slipt summat into Hepsabah's hand 'at made her e'en sparkle.

Mally gave all th' praise to Peter, for shoo sed 'at Sammy had allus befoortime landed hooam ashamed to be seen, but this time he wor a credit to her. Shoo'd noa fault to find wi' him except he should ha written ofter, an' shoo wor rayther surprised 'at th' end ov his nooas should be soa sunburned when he'd been livin' on watter.

An' soa, nah, his Yottin' trip is ended; an' aw hooap at them 'at's foller'd it will have noa reason to regret it. Partings are said to be sweet sorrow, an' that's true. But th' time has come when we mun say

### GOOD-BYE.

GOOD-BYE,—old friends,—I've had my say,
And many a long and weary day,—
And many a dark and dreary night
May pass before again I write;
    Old friends,—good-bye.

Yet still, whilst life is mine to boast,
I ne'er shall count the pleasures lost;
For in my inmost soul are set
Remembrances I'll ne'er forget,
    Old friends,—good-bye.

The snows of age may o'er us fall,
Yet oft our memory shall recall
Some treasured word or kindly deed
That soothed us in our hour of need
    Old friends,—good-bye.

And oft the tear will gently flow,
When from the page of long ago,

We call to mind the sleeping dead,
And see them as when last they said,
   "Good-bye,—good-bye."

And think of promises we made,—
Of warnings we have ne'er obeyed,—
Resolves formed o'er the open grave,
Buried beneath life's troubled wave.
   And heave a sigh.

Perchance you ne'er may think of me,
Who humbly courts your sympathy,
To draw the tear, or raise the smile,
And with my pen your hours beguile,
   Yet still,—good-bye.

These are, 'tis true, but simple words,
Yet oft a pleasure it affords,
When battling with a world of toil,
To call to mind some kindly smile,
   Some fond good-bye.

The time will come, when on the strand
Of vast Eternity we stand;
All partings over,—joy and peace
Welcome the weary soul's release,
   To rest on high.

And if no more on earth we meet
Or hold again communion sweet,—
Pray God! we meet upon that shore
Where tears are wiped, and friends no more
   Need say, good-bye.

---

W. NICHOLSON AND SONS, PRINTERS, WAKEFIELD.

www.ingramcontent.com/pod-product-compliance
Lightning Source LLC
Chambersburg PA
CBHW030311170426
43202CB00009B/962